GCSE Drama

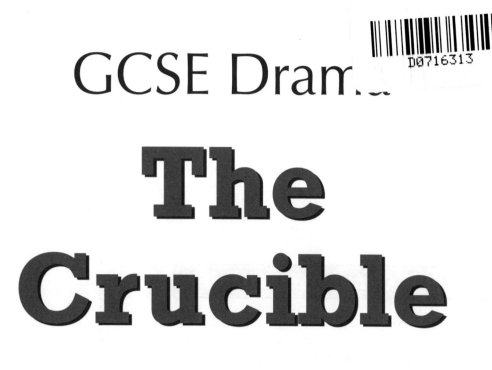

The Crucible

by Arthur Miller

Rumours, hysteria and a whole lot of get-witch-quick schemes...
life in Salem is one drama after another.

Luckily, this CGP Play Guide makes answering questions about *The Crucible*
much less of a trial. It explains everything you need to know for GCSE Drama,
from design to character performance to context.

You can test what you've learned with plenty of practice questions, and there's a
whole section of advice to help you polish up your answers in the exams.
Even John Proctor would confess this is the best guide out there.

The Play Guide

CONTENTS

CONTENTS

Section Four — Staging and Design

Section Five — Close Analysis

Section Six — Exam Advice

The Characters in 'The Crucible'
'The Crucible' Cartoon

Published by CGP

Editors:
Emma Cleasby
Zoe Fenwick
Catherine Heygate
Josh James
Kathryn Kaiser
Louise McEvoy
Holly Robinson
James Summersgill
Jack Tooth
Matt Topping

Contributors:
Mark Bennett
Paula Lunn

With thanks to Heather Cowley and Gill Stoker for the proofreading.
With thanks to Emily Smith for the copyright research.

Acknowledgements:

With thanks to Geraint Lewis for permission to use the image on the cover and the image on page 4.

With thanks to Rex Features for permission to use the images on pages 2, 3, 29, 49, 54, 57, 59, 65, 69 & 71.

Image on page 1 © Look and Learn.

Images on pages 3, 21, 24, 32, 37, 39, 40, 42, 51, 56, 58 & 64 © Drew Farrell / Royal Lyceum Theatre.

Images on pages 3, 46 & 67 © Jon Gardiner / PlayMakers Repertory Company.

With thanks to Photostage for permission to use the images on pages 3, 4, 5, 9, 18, 19, 22, 25, 30, 31, 33, 35, 36, 38, 47, 50, 52, 55, 61 & 66.

Images on pages 5, 7 & 23 © Karli Cadel / The Glimmerglass Festival.

With thanks to Alamy for permission to use the images on pages 8, 10, 28, 34, 41 & 48.

Images on pages 11, 12, 15, 20, 43, 53 & 60 © CATHERINE ASHMORE.

With thanks to Getty Images for permission to use the images on pages 13 & 14.

With thanks to Oxford Theatre Guild and Felicity Peacock for permission to use the images on pages 68 & 70. Production director: Sue Baxter.

ISBN: 978 1 78294 965 7
Printed by Elanders Ltd, Newcastle upon Tyne.
Clipart from Corel®

Based on the classic CGP style created by Richard Parsons.

Introduction to 'The Crucible'

'The Crucible' was written by Arthur Miller

1) _The Crucible_ was written in America in the 1950s, but it's set in the 17th century.

2) It's one of many plays written by Arthur Miller, a famous American playwright (see p.12-13).

3) The play is a tragedy — it has serious themes and the story follows the downfall of the play's main character, John Proctor.

4) It's also a historical drama, which means that the characters and action in the play are based on real people and real events.

> **_The Crucible_ on Stage**
>
> Directors need to know the key features of _The Crucible_ before they produce the play on stage. Aspects like the play's 17th-century setting and its genres might influence how the play is performed and designed.

The plot is based on real witch-hunts

1) _The Crucible_ tells the story of witch trials in Salem village in America in 1692.

2) Although it's based on real events and real people, it's a fictional account of what happened.

> **What really happened in 1692**
>
> - In February 1692, several girls in Salem started having fits and accused other villagers of bewitching them.
> - Over the next eight months, over 150 people were arrested for witchcraft. 19 of them were hanged.

© Look and Learn

3) Miller chose to write about the Salem witch trials because they shared similarities with modern-day witch-hunts that were happening in America when he was writing (see p.10-11). Both sets of witch-hunts were motivated by fear and paranoia.

4) This is the play's subtext — it was too dangerous for Miller to criticise the modern-day witch-hunts directly, so he wrote about Salem instead and allowed audiences to make the connection.

5) Miller also used the Salem witch trials to make a wider point about how easily lies and fear can spread in any society.

It's a play about fear and intolerance

Many of the play's themes focus on how people behave and the consequences of their actions:

1) **Fear** — Miller shows that fear brings out the worst in people and causes them to lose common sense.

2) **Intolerance** — Anyone who doesn't conform to the Church's rules is seen as a threat to Salem's society. The play criticises Salem's religious intolerance, suggesting that it leads to lies and injustice.

3) **Identity and reputation** — Miller demonstrates the struggle between trying to maintain a good reputation whilst acting in a way that is morally right. This conflict makes it hard for characters to be individuals.

4) **Envy and revenge** — Seeking revenge and acting out of jealousy is shown to be destructive.

> Directors should consider the themes they want to emphasise when making production decisions. For example, having church bells tolling periodically throughout the play would remind the audience of the way the Church dominates life in Salem. This could hint at Salem's religious intolerance.

Introduction to 'The Crucible'

Miller altered real events for dramatic effect

1) Miller made <u>changes</u> to the real events of the Salem witch trials to make sure the story '<u>worked</u>' as a piece of drama on stage.

2) For example, he <u>invented</u> the <u>affair</u> between Proctor and Abigail. This <u>sub-plot</u> makes the play more <u>interesting</u>. The affair also suggests John is <u>flawed</u>, which makes him seem more <u>human</u>.

Miller's changes make the world of the play more vivid, allowing the atmosphere of fear and distrust to seem very real to the audience. This could help a director to communicate the subtext of the play (see p.11) more effectively.

3) Miller <u>raised</u> Abigail's <u>age</u> from 11 to 17 and <u>lowered</u> John Proctor's age to make their affair <u>plausible</u>.

4) The <u>number of girls</u> making accusations was <u>reduced</u>, so that <u>fewer actors</u> would be needed overall.

5) The original Salem trials had several judges. Miller simplified the plot by <u>condensing</u> these into two characters — <u>Hathorne</u> and <u>Danforth</u>.

6) He also <u>accelerated</u> the <u>timeline</u> to increase the <u>pace</u> of the action. In <u>1692</u>, Martha, Rebecca and John were hanged on <u>separate occasions</u>, but in the <u>play</u> they are all hanged <u>together</u>.

Historical Accuracy

Many editions of the play include a <u>note</u> written by Miller on the <u>historical accuracy</u> of the <u>plot</u>. In it, Miller says he tried to present the "<u>essential nature</u>" of the Salem witch trials, despite the <u>changes</u> he made to the real events.

'The Crucible' still appeals to audiences today

1) *The Crucible* is one of Miller's most <u>successful</u> plays. The play is <u>still popular</u> in the 21st century — in <u>2016</u>, it returned to Broadway in New York for the <u>sixth</u> time.

2) Although the play is set in the 17th century, many of its ideas are <u>universal</u>. For example, Miller <u>warns</u> the audience of the <u>dangerous</u> influence that <u>fear</u> and <u>suspicion</u> can have on a person's <u>actions</u>. This <u>message</u> is still relevant today.

3) The <u>dramatic features</u> of *The Crucible* make it <u>entertaining</u>. The <u>storyline</u> is both <u>serious</u> and <u>exciting</u> — people's lives are in <u>danger</u>, and no-one knows who might be <u>accused</u> next.

4) The plot is <u>fast paced</u>, which keeps the audience <u>gripped</u>. By the end of Act Two, one <u>false rumour</u> has led to the <u>arrest</u> of <u>dozens</u> of villagers, and <u>more than 100</u> have <u>confessed</u> to witchcraft by the end of Act Four.

There have been many adaptations

You won't have to write about adaptations in your exam, but it's useful to see how the play has been presented in different ways — directors often use other works for inspiration.

1) *The Crucible* was performed in America for the <u>first time</u> in <u>1953</u> at the Martin Beck Theatre on <u>Broadway</u> (see p.15). Since then, there have been lots of <u>adaptations</u> of the play.

Abigail and Proctor in the 1996 film.

© JOHN HISCOCK/REX/Shutterstock

2) There have been multiple <u>film</u> versions. The most famous starred Daniel Day-Lewis and Winona Ryder in 1996. Miller wrote the <u>screenplay</u> for this version and was <u>closely involved</u> with the film's production.

3) The play has also been adapted into an <u>opera</u> — it was first performed by the <u>New York City Opera</u> in 1961. Its plot follows Miller's original story, but the <u>language</u> of the play was <u>rewritten</u> by the composer to <u>fit</u> with his <u>music</u>.

4) In 2014, the <u>Scottish Ballet</u> adapted the play for <u>dance</u>. Its music includes an <u>orchestral sound track</u> and <u>electronic dance</u> pieces.

Who's Who in 'The Crucible'

John Proctor...

...is a well-respected local farmer. He had an affair with Abigail, which he still feels guilty about.

Elizabeth Proctor...

...is John's wife. She's still loyal to him despite the affair, but she can't forget about it.

Reverend Parris...

...is the minister of Salem. He's more worried about money and his career than about God.

Abigail Williams...

...is Parris's niece. She's still in love with John — and she's prepared to do anything to win him back.

Reverend Hale...

...is a witchcraft expert who's called in to examine the girls.

Mary Warren...

...is a shy girl who works for the Proctors. She's friends with Abigail.

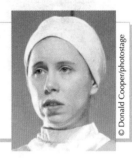

Deputy-Governor Danforth...

...is the judge in charge of the witchcraft trials. He's obsessed with his job and reputation.

The Putnams...

...are a local couple who own a lot of land. They think other people are out to get them.

Rebecca Nurse...

...is a local farmer's wife. She's known for her goodness and courage.

Giles Corey...

...is a local farmer who's had arguments with the Putnams over land. He's not afraid to speak his mind.

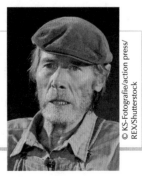

Introduction

Plot Summary

© Geraint Lewis

'The Crucible'... what happens when?

Here's a little recap of the main events of *The Crucible*. It's a good idea to learn what happens when, so that you can consider how elements of performance and design might change as the plot progresses.

Act One — Reverend Parris's house, spring 1692

- Reverend Parris caught his daughter Betty and niece Abigail dancing in the woods with his slave Tituba and some of the other village girls. Now Betty is ill. Parris accuses Abigail of conjuring spirits.

© Donald Cooper/photostage

- Abigail threatens to hurt the girls if they tell anyone that she drank a potion to kill John Proctor's wife, Elizabeth.

- John Proctor comes in. He had an affair with Abigail when she was his servant, but it's over. Abigail tells him Betty's illness isn't caused by witchcraft.

- Reverend Hale, a witchcraft 'expert', arrives.

- Abigail accuses Tituba of summoning the Devil. Tituba confesses and starts accusing others.

- Abigail and Betty claim to have seen people with the Devil.

Act Two — the Proctors' house, a week later

- The witchcraft trials have started. Elizabeth believes that John can stop the trials by telling the court that Abigail is lying, but John is reluctant.

- The Proctors' servant, Mary Warren, returns from Salem — thirty-nine women are in jail for witchcraft. Elizabeth's name has been mentioned in court. Mary gives Elizabeth a doll she's made.

© Donald Cooper/photostage

- Reverend Hale arrives to question Elizabeth.

- Giles Corey and Francis Nurse burst in — their wives have been arrested.

- Two court officials arrest Elizabeth — Abigail claims Elizabeth's spirit stuck a needle in her.

- John tells Mary she must tell the court that Abigail is lying.

Plot Summary

Act Three — the court scene

- John Proctor takes Mary Warren to court to tell the judges that the girls are lying.

- Danforth, the main judge, tells John that Elizabeth is pregnant and won't be hanged.

- Lots of villagers have signed a testimony to say that Elizabeth, Martha Corey and Rebecca Nurse aren't witches. Danforth orders everyone who signed it to be arrested.

- Mary tells the court the girls are pretending to be bewitched. They start pretending that Mary has bewitched them.

© Karli Cadel/The Glimmerglass Festival

- John admits to his affair with Abigail to ruin her reputation. Elizabeth's brought in and asked if it's true. She denies it, which destroys John's case against Abigail.

- The girls pretend that Mary's spirit is attacking them. She breaks down and accuses John of doing the Devil's work. John is arrested.

Act Four — Salem jail, autumn 1692

- Hale and Parris are persuading the prisoners to confess. Abigail has robbed Parris and vanished.

- The judges ask Elizabeth to persuade John to confess. She agrees to speak to him, but she won't promise to try to persuade him.

© Donald Cooper/photostage

- Over a hundred people have confessed. Giles Corey wouldn't plead guilty or not guilty, so he was tortured to death.

- John confesses, but he refuses to say he's seen other prisoners with the Devil.

- John tears up his confession. He's led out to be hanged.

- Parris and Hale ask Elizabeth to persuade John to confess again, but she refuses.

Think that's the end of this book? That's witchful thinking...

So... directors producing *The Crucible* have quite a lot to consider. It's a fictional play based on real 17th-century events, but it also relates to 20th-century events, and is still relevant today. If all that makes sense, reward yourself with a cuppa and go on to Section One. If you're still hazy on the plot, check out the cartoon at the back of the book.

Introduction

Life in Salem in the 17th Century

Life was tough in 17th-century Salem — living in a small gossipy town with a bad food supply, no fun or games allowed and seriously nosy neighbours must have been a pretty rough way to grow up...

Salem is a village in Massachusetts

The Crucible is set in the 17th century in the American village of <u>Salem</u>, which was founded in <u>1626</u> by a group of <u>English settlers</u>. In <u>1692</u>, Salem had about 150 houses — here are some <u>key locations</u> in the play:

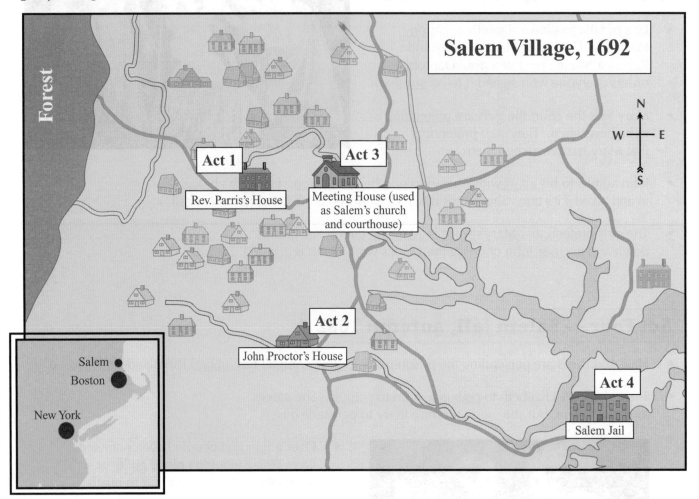

Puritans led strict and dutiful lives

1) The settlers who built Salem were <u>Puritans</u> — devout <u>Christians</u> who had <u>broken away</u> from the Church of England. In the 17th century, many Puritans travelled to America to start a <u>new life</u>.

2) Their lifestyle was <u>simple</u>. They believed people should be <u>modest</u> and <u>work hard</u>. Puritans were also <u>serious</u> — they saw <u>entertainment</u> as <u>sinful</u>, so they <u>banned</u> fun pastimes like <u>games</u> and <u>dancing</u>.

3) <u>Religion</u> was at the centre of life in Salem and the Puritans <u>dedicated their lives</u> to being good Christians. They greatly feared <u>hell</u> and thought that <u>the Devil</u> was always trying to <u>corrupt</u> them.

A costume designer might design modest outfits for the characters to show the simple and serious nature of their lifestyle.

Religion

When times were tough, the villagers in Salem thought they'd been <u>cursed</u> by <u>the Devil</u>, because they <u>couldn't explain</u> why bad things were happening to good people. Life was often hard for them — the land was harsh so their crops <u>didn't always grow</u>, Native Americans frequently <u>attacked the settlement</u> and they suffered outbreaks of <u>smallpox</u>. These hardships reinforced their <u>fear</u> and <u>belief</u> in the Devil.

Life in Salem in the 17th Century

Puritan settlements were short on luxury

1) <u>Buildings</u> in Salem were constructed from materials the settlers could find from <u>the land</u>, like <u>timber</u>.

2) Houses would have had <u>little decoration</u> and furniture would have been <u>practical</u> rather than <u>comfortable</u>.

3) Puritan <u>churches</u> were meant to be <u>plain</u> and <u>humble</u>, so the congregation could focus on <u>prayer</u> without <u>distraction</u>. Luxury was <u>disliked</u> — this is shown in Act Two when John Proctor <u>objects</u> to Parris having "<u>golden</u> candlesticks" in his "<u>clapboard</u> meetin' houses".

Set Design

A designer might use the play's <u>context</u> to make the <u>setting</u> seem more <u>authentic</u> to the audience. Salem's <u>simple</u> architecture is often reflected in the <u>set design</u> of the play.

Community was important in Salem

Everyone knew each other's business in Salem. A director could recreate this claustrophobic atmosphere by using a cramped performance space.

1) The settlers of Salem were a small, <u>isolated</u> group of people living a <u>tough life</u>. These shared hardships created a strong <u>sense of community</u>.

2) The community was a <u>theocracy</u> — a society where people see God as their ruler. This means Salem's <u>laws</u> would have closely followed the <u>religious laws</u> in the Bible.

3) In a theocracy, the laws are usually <u>enforced</u> by people who are seen to be <u>guided by God</u>, such as <u>Reverend Parris</u>. This gave some members of the community a lot of <u>power</u>.

Being different was dangerous

1) Miller uses Salem's society to show the audience how <u>dangerous</u> it can be when <u>religious intolerance</u> and <u>fear</u> of <u>difference</u> take over people's common sense.

2) In the play, anyone who <u>challenges</u> the <u>authority</u> of people like Reverend Parris is <u>mistrusted</u>, because they are suggesting that <u>God</u> can be <u>challenged</u>.

3) If someone <u>doesn't behave</u> as the church tells them to, people think <u>the Devil</u> has <u>corrupted</u> them. This leads to <u>lies</u> and <u>secrets</u>, because people are scared of being <u>judged</u> by their <u>neighbours</u> and by <u>God</u>.

4) For example, a <u>small lie</u> about <u>dancing in the woods</u> becomes <u>many big lies</u> about <u>witchcraft</u> and <u>curses</u>, because the girls are <u>too scared</u> to <u>tell the truth</u>.

© Karli Cadel/The Glimmerglass Festival

This 2016 production included a flashback to the girls dancing in the woods. The darkness on stage highlights the secretive nature of their gathering.

Reputation

- <u>Reputations</u> are important in Salem. If <u>one member</u> of the community seems to be <u>offending God</u>, the rest of the group fears for their <u>collective reputation</u>, so they <u>cast them out</u>.
- <u>Reverend Parris</u> is more concerned about his <u>reputation</u> than he is about <u>Betty's health</u> (see p.37).
- <u>Abigail</u> already can't get a job because of the <u>rumours</u> about the <u>affair</u> — if the town knew she'd tried to <u>curse</u> Elizabeth, she'd be <u>ruined</u>. She <u>accuses others</u> of witchcraft to <u>protect her reputation</u>.

Working the land probably gave them a Pure-tan...

You'll have to refer to the historical context of the play in the exam — you might want to consider how design decisions in a production of *The Crucible* could be influenced by the settlers' culture and lifestyle.

Witchcraft

Nowadays when you think of magic, you might imagine an old bearded guy with a big stick or a teenager with glasses and a scar, but witchcraft was a serious and deadly business in the 17th century...

The Salem witch trials really happened

1) *The Crucible* is based on a set of real witch trials that took place in Salem in the 17th century. In 1692, three Salem women were accused of witchcraft by Abigail Williams and Betty Parris.

2) It was easy for the people of Salem to believe that these three women were witches because they were different — Sarah Good was a beggar, Tituba was a black slave and Sarah Osburn didn't go to church.

3) They were arrested and put on trial. These trials led to more accusations, eventually causing mass hysteria. Over 150 people in Salem were accused of witchcraft before the panic died down.

4) Witchcraft was a very serious charge in 17th-century Salem. It was almost impossible to prove your innocence, and if you didn't confess you would be hanged. 26 people were put on trial and all of them were found guilty. 19 were hanged.

Making the play's settings and characters seem authentic to the 17th century could help to remind the audience that the play is based on real events.

The Puritans associated witches with the Devil

1) The Puritans believed that a witch was someone who had given their soul over to the Devil, and that the Devil gave witches supernatural powers.

2) They thought the Devil encouraged witches to corrupt others — in Act Three, Mary accuses Proctor of coming to her "by night and every day" to make her sign her name in "the Devil's book".

3) This is why the trials progressed quickly. The judges wanted to stop witchcraft from spreading.

Witch Trials

1) Accused witches were put on trial in the hope that they would confess and reveal other witches in the community.

2) Some people who refused to confess were tortured. This is what happens to Giles Corey — he's pressed under heavy stones.

3) Those who confessed weren't executed, but could lose their land and property, and were usually excluded from the church and the community.

© Archive PL / Alamy Stock Photo

A sketch of Giles Corey being pressed.

Anyone could be accused of witchcraft

In the Bible, Eve is tempted by the Devil to disobey God, causing humans to be cast out of the Garden of Eden. The people of Salem would have known this story, and it would have influenced their view of women.

1) The Puritans believed that women were weaker than men, so they would give in more easily to the temptations of the Devil. This meant that women were more frequently accused — but men could be witches too.

2) Anyone who acted in a way the church disapproved of was in danger of being accused. For example, in the play John forgets one of the Ten Commandments, which makes Reverend Hale suspicious of his "Christian character".

3) Although at first those accused were women of low status like Tituba and Sarah Good, even respected members of the community like Rebecca Nurse were arrested and hanged.

Performance

The girls discover that accusing people of witchcraft gives them more power and status. Performers could show this change through their posture by standing tall and proud from Act Two onwards.

Witchcraft

In the play, rumours of witchcraft are spread by fear

1) The <u>rumours</u> about witchcraft are '<u>confirmed</u>' by the girls in Act One, who <u>lie</u> because they're <u>afraid</u> they'll get into <u>trouble</u> for dancing — they seize the chance to <u>blame other people</u> for their behaviour.

2) <u>Fear</u> keeps the rumours of witchcraft <u>alive</u>. Some people give <u>fake confessions</u> to save themselves, and then <u>accuse others</u> of corrupting them. This is what <u>Tituba</u> does in Act One when she's told she must either <u>confess</u> or be <u>whipped to death</u>.

3) <u>Fear</u> makes people <u>hysterical</u> — people abandon their <u>common sense</u> and get <u>swept up</u> in the excitement. This is seen in Act Three when <u>Mary Warren</u> tries to admit that the accusations were <u>lies</u>. When the other girls <u>turn on her</u> and insist they can see a 'bird', she becomes <u>convinced</u> that she can see it too.

© Donald Cooper/photostage

The Bird

The bird gives the <u>director</u> a dilemma — showing the <u>bird</u> on stage would help the audience to <u>understand</u> Mary's fear, but it needs to be clear that the bird <u>isn't real</u>. Directors need to convey the <u>genuine fear</u> of witchcraft without suggesting that it <u>exists</u>.

The trials are used to settle old scores

1) The Puritans' <u>Christian</u> values would have <u>discouraged</u> the villagers from <u>taking revenge publicly</u> on others, so some characters see the trials as a <u>convenient</u> opportunity to act on old <u>grudges</u>.

2) <u>Jealousy</u> is also an underlying motive in the play. Life can be <u>hard</u> in Salem, so when some villagers are <u>more fortunate</u> than others, people become <u>envious</u> of their good luck. This envy <u>influences</u> the way some characters <u>respond</u> to witchcraft in Salem.

Envy and Revenge

- Abigail is <u>jealous</u> of <u>Elizabeth</u> because Elizabeth is John's wife. Abigail is also <u>angry</u> at being <u>sacked</u> by her. She uses the trials to <u>punish</u> Elizabeth.
- Abigail also uses the trials to <u>take revenge</u> on the rest of the village for <u>gossiping</u> about her.
- The accusations made by the <u>Putnams</u> might be motivated by <u>jealousy</u> and <u>revenge</u> too — in his background notes (see p.23) Miller says that the Putnams have had <u>disputes</u> with the Nurses <u>over land</u> in the past. Later in the play, they claim that <u>Rebecca Nurse</u> caused the <u>cot deaths</u> of their <u>children</u>, and Giles accuses Thomas Putnam of "<u>reaching out</u> for land".

3) Miller establishes <u>resentment</u> between the villagers from the <u>outset</u> of the play — it's important for a production to show there is <u>conflict</u> between the villagers <u>before</u> the accusations start. In Act One, actors playing Parris and Proctor could <u>face</u> each other with <u>closed body language</u> to make their <u>hostility</u> clear.

GCSEs may be a trial, but this page is pure magic...

Imagine that you are a Puritan in 17th-century Salem and have been falsely accused of witchcraft. Write a paragraph explaining your reaction, including:

1) What you think will happen to you now that you've been accused.

2) Whether or not you will confess and why.

Putting yourself in the same situation as the accused characters in the play could give you ideas on how to direct or perform these characters.

The USA and Communism in the 1950s

So why would a playwright in 1950s America decide to write a play about witch-hunts from 300 years ago? It's all to do with communist witch-hunts. Wait, more witch-hunts? Which witch-hunts? Oh dear...

The USA was afraid of communism

1) The USA is capitalist. In capitalist countries, most businesses are privately owned and mainly free from government interference. People work to make their own money and can build their own businesses.

2) Communism is the opposite of capitalism. The theory of communism is that everyone is equal and private ownership isn't allowed.

3) In the first half of the 20th century, many Americans feared communism. They saw it as a threat to their freedom and their ability to own and control their property.

The Cold War increased people's fears

1) After World War Two, the USSR (which included modern-day Russia) had become a communist superpower. America was afraid that the USSR would try to spread communist ideas around the world.

2) The USA had also become a superpower, so the USSR feared worldwide American influence. These tensions led to the Cold War.

A superpower is a country with a strong military and economy. It has a lot of power and political influence.

- The Cold War was a period of intense rivalry and competition between the USA and the USSR (and their allies) which lasted for over 40 years. They competed with each other to have the best economy, strongest military and greatest political influence.

- It was a period of great worry and suspicion — both countries had nuclear weapons capable of causing mass destruction, and they lived in constant fear of being attacked by the other side.

- Each side used propaganda (one-sided information designed to mislead others) to build hysteria that the other side was lurking everywhere. In the USA, this increased panic about communism.

America carried out real-life 'witch-hunts'

The hysteria about communism during the McCarthy era was similar to the hysteria about witchcraft that Miller wrote about in The Crucible — people were paranoid.

1) As anti-communist hysteria grew in America, the government wanted to find potential communists and stop them from spreading their views.

2) The House Un-American Activities Committee (HUAC) was a US government body that was very influential at the time. It investigated people and organisations that were believed to have links to communism (see p.13 for Miller's own experience of HUAC).

3) HUAC used intimidation and the threat of imprisonment to try to make people confess.

4) In the 1950s, Senator Joseph McCarthy campaigned against communism in America, claiming that communists had secretly entered the US government.

5) McCarthy hunted out communists and was supported by many influential politicians. Like HUAC, he was known for his aggressive questioning techniques and for accusing people with little evidence.

6) Naming someone as a communist could ruin their reputation — most of the people who were accused lost their jobs or were imprisoned.

7) Those arrested were encouraged to accuse friends and colleagues in return for their release, which created distrust and paranoia.

8) These proceedings were labelled 'witch-hunts' because people were accused of crimes and punished with little or no evidence.

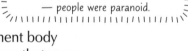
Senator McCarthy in 1954.

Section One — Context and Themes

The USA and Communism in the 1950s

The play has a lot of parallels with McCarthyism

1) Miller wrote *The Crucible* during the Cold War and McCarthy's anti-communist campaign. He portrays the injustice of the McCarthy era through the way Salem responds to witchcraft.

2) In the McCarthy era, people sometimes used an accusation of communism as a way to get revenge on someone they had a grudge against, just like Abigail uses her accusations to punish people who have been gossiping about her.

3) It was very difficult to prove that you weren't a communist once you'd been accused, in the same way that it's difficult for the characters in the play to prove they aren't witches.

4) People's reputations were often ruined by communist accusations. Similarly, both Elizabeth and Rebecca Nurse have good reputations at the start of the play, but are treated like criminals by the judges once they have been accused.

5) Lots of people in 1950s America also received fines and prison sentences for refusing to accuse others — this is what happens to Giles in Act Three. He refuses to tell Danforth who testified against the Putnams in case the accuser gets into trouble too, so Danforth arrests Giles for defying the court.

© CATHERINE ASHMORE

Performance

Miller shows how irrational the trials were by having characters with such good reputations arrested. A director might ask performers to show shock and confusion to emphasise this senselessness to the audience.

This gives the director a contextual dilemma

1) Miller would have expected his initial audiences to recognise the similarities between the witch-hunts in the play and the witch-hunts in 1950s America.

2) However, many modern audiences have not lived through McCarthyism, and might not know enough about the era to recognise the connection.

3) This presents a director of the play with a challenge:

- They can portray a realistic telling of the Salem witch trials, as Miller intended, but they risk the audience missing the full message of the play.

- Alternatively, they can make it clearer that the witch-hunts in the play are meant to be a metaphor for the anti-communist campaign in 1950s America, but this would go against Miller's original intention to create a realistic version of events.

- Both of these approaches are valid interpretations.

> The director could include references to the 1950s and communism in their production through design. For example, a set designer might place some anti-communist propaganda outside the court.

Who you gonna call? Witch-hunters...

Imagine you're a director who has decided to stage a production of 'The Crucible' set in 1950s America. Write a paragraph explaining your choice. Make sure you include:

1) Why you've chosen this setting.
2) The advantages and disadvantages of your choice of setting.
3) The effect of your setting on a modern-day audience.

Tick list:
✓ social, historical and cultural context
✓ playwright's intentions
✓ audience response

Arthur Miller

World famous with tons of successful plays — Arthur Miller is a pretty big deal in the drama world. The events he lived through had a big impact on *The Crucible*, so it's worth knowing a bit about him...

Arthur Miller was an American playwright

1) Arthur Miller was one of the most famous American playwrights of the 20th century. He also wrote many fiction books, essays and screenplays.

2) He was born in 1915 in New York, and died in 2005, aged 89.

3) His first successful play was *All My Sons* in 1947, and he became even more famous with *Death of a Salesman* two years later. His celebrity status in America grew when he married Marilyn Monroe in 1956. They divorced in 1961.

Miller's Beliefs

- Miller was interested in political and social issues. He lived through the Wall Street Crash, the Great Depression and World War Two. He saw the impact that these events had on American life and culture, which influenced his views on society.
- Miller thought that theatre should represent what life is really like, so his plays often examine the flaws in American society as well as its strengths.
- He believed that theatre was an effective way to bring people together, and that it gave him an opportunity to communicate with the public.

> The Wall Street Crash refers to when the US stock market crashed in 1929, causing severe damage to the American economy. This was followed by years of widespread unemployment and poverty known as the Great Depression.

He wrote plays about social and moral issues

1) Miller is known for writing plays that have social and political messages about life in America.

2) The issues he explores are often universal, so audiences can easily engage with them. For example, in the play, any characters who contradict Salem's rules are at risk of being accused of witchcraft. This is similar to the way that societies often struggle to accept individuals who are seen to be different.

In Act Two, Proctor knows he should tell the court the girls are lying, but he's afraid his affair will be discovered.

3) The events and characters in Miller's plays are usually realistic to help the audience relate to his heroes and their struggles.

4) Miller often chose to make his protagonists common men like John Proctor in *The Crucible*. This allows him to use that man's dilemmas to comment on wider social issues.

5) Miller also uses his plays to explore moral problems, by creating situations where it isn't easy for characters to decide what the right thing to do is. His characters then have to live with the consequences of their decisions.

6) His characters sometimes experience a moral journey. The title of *The Crucible* can be seen as a metaphor for these moral journeys — in chemistry, you put something into a crucible and heat it to a very high temperature to purify it.

> You could apply this metaphor to the experiences of John, Elizabeth and Reverend Hale — they all struggle through the moral dilemmas of the witch trials and come out of the experience as better people. The pressure of the trials can be interpreted as the 'heat' that purifies them, as it prompts them to do what they think is right rather than what is easy.

Arthur Miller

Miller was influenced by the McCarthyist era

1) After some major film industry strikes, many writers and entertainers were accused by the government of being communists during the 1940s and 1950s, when Miller was writing.

2) HUAC (the House Un-American Activities Committee) targeted the Hollywood entertainment industry because the government was worried it might make communist propaganda films. Many writers and actors were blacklisted (meaning no-one would hire them) after they refused to confess to supporting communism.

See p.10 for more on McCarthyism and HUAC.

3) As a famous figure in the entertainment industry, Miller would have witnessed first hand the anger and suspicion caused by HUAC's investigations.

4) Elia Kazan was a film director and a friend of Miller's who was questioned by HUAC in 1952 about suspected communist activity. Kazan admitted that he had been a communist in the past and gave them the names of several of his friends.

5) Miller was shocked and upset that his friend had been put on trial and that Kazan had given the court the names of their friends. The two men didn't speak for ten years afterwards — many people believe that *The Crucible* was partly inspired by this experience.

Miller became associated with communism in the 1950s

1) In 1956, three years after *The Crucible* was first performed, Miller was summoned by HUAC for questioning.

2) HUAC was interested in Miller because he had been linked to suspected communists in the past. The fact that the *The Crucible* seemed to criticise the 1950s 'witch-hunts' also made some people suspect that he supported communism.

3) During the trial, Miller refused to name anyone else as a communist, so he was convicted.

4) As a result, his passport was confiscated, he was fined and he was blacklisted. In 1958, his conviction was overturned.

5) Miller was unwilling to name other people and get them into trouble in the way that Elia Kazan had — this is the same attitude held by Giles Corey and John Proctor in *The Crucible*.

© Bettmann / Getty Images

Arthur Miller (right) testifying before HUAC in 1956.

Set Design

A director of a non-naturalistic production of the play might wish to highlight the link between Miller's own views and Proctor's by briefly projecting quotes from Miller's trial onto the backdrop when Proctor refuses to name other villagers as witches in Act Four.

Miller's Influences

The McCarthyist era influenced Miller's ideas in *The Crucible*, but it probably wasn't his only inspiration. It's worth thinking about Miller's earlier experiences too — Miller lived through World War Two, where people often collaborated with others and ignored persecution around them because they were too scared to speak out.

Knowing what inspired Miller is helpful for directors, performers and designers so they can decide which ideas they might want to highlight for the audience.

EXAM TIP

And the moral of the story is...

Miller explores ideas that lots of people can relate to — consider how a performer, designer or director might present these ideas in a production to make the play more relevant to a modern audience.

14

The Play on Stage

Now you've got to grips with the background to the events of the play, it's time to look at some theatrical context. You probably thought you were done with history, but the play has a whole history of its own...

There were two popular theatre trends in 1950s America

1) *The Crucible's* first production ran on Broadway — the main street in New York's theatre district. Theatre performed on Broadway is typically considered the best theatre in America.

2) There were two popular trends on Broadway in the post-war era — musicals like *Guys and Dolls* (1950) and *The King and I* (1951), and dramas like *A Streetcar Named Desire* (1947).

3) Musicals were usually set in faraway places, with romance, comedy and a happy ending. They provided an escape from ordinary life.

4) Dramas typically focused on American families and communities, and their behaviour towards each other. Some were quite political, like *The Crucible*, whereas others focused on how people dealt with social conflict.

Social dramas

After the war, America experienced greater social inequality than before, which made many Americans more aware of issues in society. This helped to make theatre that focused on political and social issues more popular.

Many dramas were performed in a naturalistic style

1) Naturalism is a style of theatre that aims to make the action on stage seem realistic (see p.20).

2) The style developed in the late 19th century. Konstantin Stanislavski, a Russian actor and director, helped to develop naturalistic theatre. He thought that creating believable characters would help plays to seem more real.

3) To achieve this, he developed several new techniques for actors. For example, he encouraged performers to create detailed backstories for their characters to help them understand what motivated their actions.

4) Naturalism gained popularity in America during the first half of the 20th century. People were inspired by Stanislavski's techniques — in 1931, actor Lee Strasberg helped to found the Group Theatre in New York, which produced naturalistic theatre and trained actors using methods based on Stanislavski's ideas.

5) By the 1950s, naturalism was a main influence on American theatre.

Lee Strasberg (left) directing a naturalistic performance in 1941.

There wasn't a specific set of theatre conventions in the 1950s

1) Although naturalistic conventions were popular in the first half of the 20th century, American theatre also became more experimental. A wide variety of different theatre styles and conventions had developed and were being used by the 1950s.

The theatre conventions of a certain period are the features of the style of staging, design and performance that were in use at that time.

2) This means that Miller didn't have a clear set of conventions to follow when he wrote *The Crucible* — he chose naturalistic conventions with particular intentions in mind.

Directors can choose whether or not to follow Miller's conventions in their productions. However, directors of non-naturalistic productions should still consider the effects Miller might have been trying to achieve and take these into account in their performance and design decisions.

The Play on Stage

The first production of 'The Crucible' got mixed reviews

1) *The Crucible* was first <u>performed</u> in America in January <u>1953</u> at the Martin Beck Theatre on <u>Broadway</u>.

2) The initial production received a <u>mixed</u> response — it won several <u>awards</u>, but it had a <u>relatively short run</u> of performances.

3) The <u>set</u> and <u>costume</u> designs followed Miller's <u>stage directions</u>. The <u>costumes</u> reflected the style of clothes that the <u>Puritans</u> would have worn, and the <u>set</u> used <u>plain</u>, <u>basic</u> furniture.

4) However, the director also used some <u>non-naturalistic</u> conventions, like having the actors <u>address</u> their lines to the <u>audience</u> rather than to each other. Some critics thought this made the <u>dialogue</u> seem <u>stilted</u>. The actors also <u>didn't move</u> on stage when speaking their lines, which meant the production was <u>criticised</u> for being <u>unemotional</u>.

5) After the first performances received some <u>negative reviews</u>, the <u>director</u> left and Miller tried to <u>rescue</u> the remaining performances. He <u>rewrote</u> some sections and added a <u>scene</u> at the end of <u>Act Two</u>, but even then the play didn't really take off.

Effect on the Audience

The play's <u>criticism</u> of <u>McCarthyism</u> may have made people <u>cautious</u> about <u>attending</u> a performance.

Act Two, Scene Two is not usually included in modern productions. In it, Proctor meets Abigail the night before Elizabeth's trial.

Different productions use different conventions

1) Between the <u>1950s</u> and <u>today</u>, directors of the play have <u>experimented</u> with different theatre conventions.

2) In 1958, the Martinique Theatre in New York put on an <u>in-the-round</u> performance, which may have helped the <u>audience</u> feel more <u>involved</u> in the action.

3) The production also introduced a character called '<u>the Reader</u>' to read out Miller's <u>background notes</u> from Act One (see p.23) — this gave the audience more <u>detailed information</u> on the <u>characters</u> and the <u>community</u> in Salem.

4) A 2010 production at Regent's Park Open Air Theatre in London staged the play <u>outside</u> at <u>sunset</u>, which emphasised how the <u>mood</u> of the play <u>darkens</u> as the action progresses. This increased the play's <u>threatening atmosphere</u>.

5) A 2016 Broadway production of the play left out any <u>visual links</u> to the <u>17th century</u>. <u>Separating</u> the play from a specific <u>time</u> and <u>place</u> may have helped to emphasise the play's <u>universal themes</u> to the audience.

Proctor in the Regent's Park Open Air production.

Theatrical context can affect production decisions

1) A director of *The Crucible* could use <u>previous productions</u> for <u>inspiration</u>. For example, the 1958 Martinique Theatre production might inspire a director to consider <u>ways</u> of including Miller's <u>background notes</u> in a performance.

2) Knowing what <u>critics</u> have said about <u>past productions</u> could also help a director to decide what <u>effects</u> they want to create for the <u>audience</u>. As the 1953 Broadway production was criticised for being <u>unemotional</u>, they might decide to avoid using conventions that <u>distance</u> the audience from the <u>action</u>.

3) Miller wrote *The Crucible* to be performed in a <u>professional</u> theatre like the theatres on <u>Broadway</u>. Some of Miller's more detailed <u>stage directions</u> about design, e.g. that wooden boards should "*make up the walls*" in the meeting house, might need to be <u>adapted</u> for a production in a different theatre setting.

Experimenting can lead to some interesting reactions...

The range of theatrical conventions in use in America during the 1950s meant writers were free to create whatever sort of play they wanted — consider why Miller might have chosen the conventions that he did.

Practice Questions

So you've finished your first section, but now comes the tricky part — seeing how much of it you can actually remember. Have a go at these quick questions to see how much information you've absorbed. Once you've worked through them, try to write around a paragraph for each in-depth question below.

Quick Questions

1) Give two examples of religious beliefs that the Puritans held in 17th-century Salem.

2) Explain what a theocracy is.

3) How did the Puritans in the 17th century believe that people turned into witches?

4) Give an example of when a character behaves differently to the rest of society in the play, and describe how this behaviour creates suspicion about them.

5) Who was Joseph McCarthy and what did he do?

6) Give three possible consequences of being named as a communist in the McCarthy era.

7) Why is *The Crucible* an appropriate title for the play?

8) When and where was *The Crucible* first performed in America?

9) Name two popular trends of theatre in America in the 1950s.

In-depth Questions

1) Explain how the 17th-century Puritan lifestyle might influence your costume design for Mary Warren.

2) How do the witch trials in the play link to Miller's themes of envy and revenge?

3) Why are the girls so afraid of people finding out that they danced in the woods?

4) Explain how the witch-hunts in the play can be seen as a metaphor for the communist 'witch-hunts' of the 1950s.

5) How might Miller's own experiences have influenced the plot of *The Crucible*?

6) Give two examples of theatre conventions used in the original production of the play. Would you use these conventions in a production today? Explain why/why not.

Practice Questions

Now that you've got to grips with the context of the play and its themes, you're ready to look at some exam-style questions. They're the type of higher mark questions you could get asked in the exam, so don't try to dash them off all at once — it's worth taking your time and answering each one properly.

Exam-style Questions

> Find the part of Act Two where Proctor tears up the warrant. Read from where Hale says "**Mary Warren, a needle have been found inside this poppet**" to where Proctor says "**I'll pay you, Herrick, I will surely pay you!**", then answer Question 1 below.

1) Imagine you're a designer working on *The Crucible*. Explain how you would use props and stage furniture to portray this extract effectively on stage to the audience. You should refer to the play's context in your answer.

> Read from the start of Act Three to where Danforth says "**Clear this room**", then answer Question 2 below.

2) As a designer working on a production of the play, explain how you would use staging to portray this extract effectively to the audience. You should refer to the play's context in your answer.

> Find the part of Act Three where Giles accuses Putnam of encouraging his daughter to make a false accusation. Read Act Three from where Danforth says "**Mr Putnam, I have here an accusation by Mr Corey against you**" to where Giles says "**I'll cut your throat, Putnam, I'll kill you yet!**", then answer Question 3 below.

3) Imagine you're a lighting designer working on a production of the play. Describe how you would use lighting to create effects that reinforce the action in this extract. You should explain why your ideas are suitable for this extract and for the rest of the play, and refer to the play's context in your answer.

> Find the part of Act Four where Elizabeth is brought out of jail to talk to Danforth. Read from where Parris says "**Hush!**" to where Elizabeth says "**I promise nothing. Let me speak with him**", then answer Question 4 below.

4) Imagine you're a director creating a production of *The Crucible*. Explain how a costume designer might portray this extract effectively on stage to the audience. Refer to the play's context in your answer.

Genre

Genre refers to what type of story a performance tells — each genre has its own style and features. This gives the audience an idea about what to expect from a play. If it's a tragedy, bring the tissues.

'The Crucible' is a historical drama...

© Donald Cooper/photostage

1) A <u>historical drama</u> is a story based on <u>real events</u>, using characters based on <u>real people</u>. Playwrights often <u>adapt</u> the historical events for <u>dramatic effect</u>. They might also <u>add</u>, <u>remove</u> or <u>change</u> characters to make the story work <u>on stage</u>.

2) Miller based *The Crucible* on the <u>Salem witch trials</u> in <u>1692</u> (see p.8).

3) He used these events to make the audience think about the <u>dangers</u> of fear, lies and distrust in <u>modern America</u>.

4) He wanted the play to be an '<u>honest</u>' retelling, but it <u>wasn't</u> meant to be completely historically <u>accurate</u>. Miller <u>accelerated</u> the timeline of events and <u>invented</u> the <u>affair</u> between Abigail and Proctor (see p.2).

5) Producing the play in a <u>naturalistic style</u> (see p.20) would highlight the <u>historical drama</u> genre to the audience, as it would help them to feel as though they're watching a <u>real story</u> about <u>real people</u>.

6) The historical drama genre can also be emphasised through <u>design choices</u> — e.g. by using <u>realistic 17th-century Puritan costumes</u> to reflect the play's historical setting.

... but it's also a tragedy

1) A <u>tragedy</u> is a story based on the <u>downfall</u> of the main character.

2) Like most tragedies, *The Crucible* deals with <u>serious themes</u>, has an <u>unhappy ending</u> and is <u>sad</u> for the audience to watch.

3) <u>Tragedies</u> traditionally focus on <u>high-status characters</u> like kings or princes — Miller goes <u>against</u> this in *The Crucible* by having <u>John Proctor</u>, a "*farmer in his middle thirties*", as the <u>tragic hero</u>.

4) Most tragic heroes have a key <u>flaw</u> that leads to their downfall — for Proctor, his <u>pride</u> and desire to <u>protect</u> his <u>name</u> and <u>reputation</u> lead to his death.

> **Effect on the Audience**
>
> In Act One, the other villagers could use <u>informal gestures</u>, like laying a hand on Proctor's arm, to emphasise his status as an ordinary '<u>everyman</u>' character. This would make it easier for the audience to <u>identify</u> and <u>empathise</u> with his struggles.

The play's genres have an impact on the audience

1) The fact that *The Crucible* is a <u>tragedy</u> creates an <u>expectation</u> for the <u>audience</u> — a <u>tragedy</u> typically ends with the <u>death</u> of the main character.

2) A <u>tragedy</u> should cause the audience to experience <u>strong emotions</u> — the release of these emotions is called <u>catharsis</u>. In *The Crucible*, the audience might feel <u>scared</u> when innocent people are arrested and then feel <u>sorrow</u> when they're hanged. <u>Experiencing</u> these emotions allows the audience to <u>get rid</u> of them.

3) As a <u>historical drama</u>, the play may have a powerful impact on the audience because they know that the events happened to <u>real people</u>. This could help them to <u>sympathise</u> with the characters' <u>suffering</u>.

4) The <u>combination</u> of the two genres shows the audience how <u>real-life events</u> can be <u>tragic</u>. Miller perhaps wanted the audience to consider whether <u>McCarthyism</u> in <u>1950s America</u> (see p.10-11) was <u>tragic</u>.

My love life — a historical drama and a tragedy...

In the exam, it won't be enough to just write that the play is a historical drama and a tragedy — you need to be ready to explain how these genres might affect choices made by a director, designer or performer.

Structure

Directors need to consider structure too — no-one wants to hear relaxing music at a really tense moment.

The play follows a tragic structure

There are <u>five parts</u> to the structure of a typical <u>tragedy</u>:

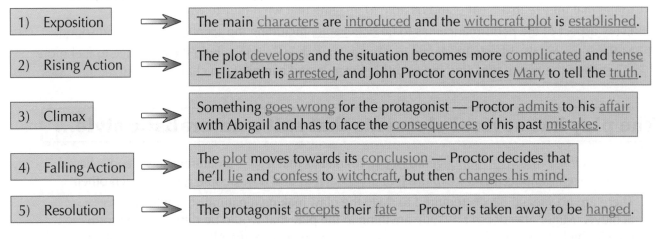

1) Exposition ⟹	The main <u>characters</u> are <u>introduced</u> and the <u>witchcraft plot</u> is <u>established</u>.
2) Rising Action ⟹	The plot <u>develops</u> and the situation becomes more <u>complicated</u> and <u>tense</u> — Elizabeth is <u>arrested</u>, and John Proctor convinces <u>Mary</u> to tell the <u>truth</u>.
3) Climax ⟹	Something <u>goes wrong</u> for the protagonist — Proctor <u>admits</u> to his <u>affair</u> with Abigail and has to face the <u>consequences</u> of his past <u>mistakes</u>.
4) Falling Action ⟹	The <u>plot</u> moves towards its <u>conclusion</u> — Proctor decides that he'll <u>lie</u> and <u>confess</u> to <u>witchcraft</u>, but then <u>changes his mind</u>.
5) Resolution ⟹	The protagonist <u>accepts</u> their <u>fate</u> — Proctor is taken away to be <u>hanged</u>.

The action is fast paced

1) Miller <u>condenses</u> the historical events into roughly <u>3 months</u> and tells the story in <u>chronological order</u>. These features <u>speed up</u> the action and create a sense that the play is heading <u>unavoidably</u> towards its <u>tragic end</u>.

2) Each act has only one <u>scene</u> and one <u>setting</u>, ensuring that the audience's <u>attention</u> during each act is never <u>interrupted</u>.

3) The <u>speed</u> of the action in the first two acts is very <u>quick</u> — it only takes a <u>week</u> after the girls are caught dancing for nearly <u>40 people</u> to be <u>arrested</u>.

4) This creates <u>tension</u> for the audience as it appears as though people are <u>acting rashly</u> and the action is spiralling <u>out of control</u>.

5) The play <u>isn't</u> in a <u>constant</u> state of <u>high tension</u> — the action <u>steadily increases</u> to a <u>climax</u> at the end of each act. This structure means that the audience aren't <u>numbed</u> by <u>constant drama</u>.

John's arrest in Act Three shows how hasty the trials have become.

Entrances and exits are carefully planned

1) The play is <u>full</u> of characters <u>entering</u> or <u>exiting</u> — this can <u>create</u> or <u>relieve tension</u>.

2) For example, in Act Two, Mary's entrance <u>breaks</u> the building tension of the Proctors' argument, allowing the tension to be <u>rebuilt</u> as the act progresses. In contrast, Hale's <u>sudden entrance</u> raises the tension as it is <u>unexpected</u>.

3) In Act Three, <u>Parris's exit</u> from the stage creates <u>tension</u> — the audience <u>know</u> that he will <u>return</u> at some point with Elizabeth, but they <u>don't know when</u>, or what <u>Elizabeth</u> will <u>say</u> when she's asked about her husband's affair.

> A director must think carefully about Hale's entrance in Act Two. He appears "as though from the air" — the performer must appear suddenly to surprise the audience.

Blink and you'll miss it — things happen fast in Salem...

Think about how Miller has structured the play and why things happen when they do. There's usually a good reason why a certain character appears, disappears or says something at a particular moment.

Style

Style is all about how a play is produced. Which is a good job really, because I know nothing about fashion...

'The Crucible' is often staged in a naturalistic style

1) <u>Naturalism</u> is a style of theatre that aims to recreate <u>real life</u> on stage. The audience should <u>forget</u> that they're in a <u>theatre</u> and be able to <u>imagine</u> that what they're watching is <u>real</u>.

2) Every aspect of the performance has to be <u>believable</u>, including the <u>scenery</u>, <u>lighting</u> and <u>sound</u>.

3) Miller <u>intended</u> the play to be staged in a <u>naturalistic style</u> — it may help the audience to feel more <u>invested</u> in the play if they find the events <u>believable</u> and can <u>relate</u> to characters like the Proctors.

The play has several elements that suit a naturalistic style...

1) *The Crucible's* <u>historical drama</u> genre (see p.18) means that it <u>suits</u> a naturalistic style. It's based on <u>real events</u> and its themes explore <u>human behaviour</u> and how people <u>relate</u> to each other.

2) There are no <u>special effects</u> required to stage the play, making a naturalistic style easy to achieve. Miller also <u>doesn't include</u> anything in the play that would be <u>difficult</u> to perform <u>convincingly</u> on stage. For example, the <u>hangings</u> at the end of the play take place <u>offstage</u>.

3) The <u>language</u> of the play (see p.24-25) is meant to echo <u>17th-century speech</u>, which makes the audience feel as though they're watching events from <u>that time</u>.

> **Vocal Skills**
>
> In a naturalistic production, actors have to make it <u>seem</u> as though they're talking <u>naturally</u> to each other. But they still need to <u>project</u> their voices so that the audience can <u>hear</u>. This could be <u>challenging</u> at times, e.g. in Act One where Abigail <u>whispers</u> "Not I, sir" to Parris.

... and Miller gives instructions about how to achieve this style

1) Miller wrote <u>detailed stage directions</u> (see p.22-23) to create a <u>realistic impression</u> of 17th-century Salem.

2) Each of the four <u>settings</u> is intended to look like a <u>real place</u>, with realistic <u>props</u>. The stage directions at the start of Act Two describe the Proctors' "*common room*" as a "*rather long living room of the time*" and John Proctor takes a "*pot*" out of the <u>fire</u>. This creates the impression of a functioning <u>family home</u>.

3) Miller also includes stage directions about the <u>lighting</u> to create a naturalistic effect. He suggests imitating naturalistic sources of light such as the "*morning <u>sunlight</u>*" in Act One and the "*fire*" in Act Two to create an <u>authentic</u> atmosphere on stage.

© CATHERINE ASHMORE

Realistic costumes are also important for achieving a naturalistic style.

> **Non-naturalistic Style**
>
> Miller's instructions are only for <u>guidance</u> — a director can choose to stage *The Crucible* in a <u>non-naturalistic style</u>. Non-naturalistic theatre includes features that <u>remind</u> an audience that what they're watching <u>isn't real</u>. Flick to Section Four for some different examples of <u>non-naturalistic elements</u> that could be used in a production of the play.

The play's style was so naturalistic I forgot I was revising...

When writing about the extract in the exam, make sure that you consider Miller's naturalistic style. You don't have to stick to it, but you do have to explain why you'd stage the production in a particular way.

Mood and Atmosphere

The Crucible is full of fear and tension. The mood and atmosphere of a production should reflect this.

The setting creates a claustrophobic atmosphere

1) The play is <u>set</u> in Salem — it's a small community where everyone knows everyone's business. This creates a sense that the characters are always being <u>watched</u>.

2) Each act is set in a <u>single room</u> — a <u>bedroom</u>, a <u>living room</u>, a room at the <u>court</u> and a <u>prison cell</u>. Setting the play in such <u>confined spaces</u> creates a <u>claustrophobic</u> mood and suggests the characters are <u>unable</u> to <u>escape</u> their <u>fates</u>.

3) In Act One, <u>Tituba's confession</u> to Parris and Hale is also <u>observed</u> by Giles, Rebecca and the Putnams. Having her <u>surrounded</u> on stage by lots of other characters helps to create an atmosphere of <u>accusation</u> and <u>judgement</u>.

© Drew Farrell/Royal Lyceum Theatre

Elements of performance show the atmosphere of fear

The <u>stage directions</u> often describe the <u>movement</u>, <u>gestures</u> and <u>actions</u> of characters to create or reflect <u>fear</u>:

- The play's <u>opening</u> gives the audience a vivid impression of Parris's <u>confusion</u> and <u>fear</u>. The image of a grown man <u>mumbling</u>, <u>weeping</u> and desperately <u>praying</u> creates a <u>tense</u> and <u>fearful</u> atmosphere.
- In Act One, Tituba <u>breaks down</u> as she confesses, "*rocking on her knees*" and "*sobbing in terror.*" This creates an <u>uncomfortable</u> mood as it could be <u>visually disturbing</u> for the audience to watch.
- When the girls act <u>as one</u> in Act Three, it creates a <u>supernatural</u> and <u>fearful</u> atmosphere. This could also transfer to the <u>audience</u>, who may be uneasy about what the girls will <u>do next</u>.

The use of sound contributes to the mood and atmosphere

1) Elizabeth "*softly singing*" at the start of Act Two creates a <u>gentle</u> mood. This <u>contrasts</u> with the <u>frenzied atmosphere</u> at the end of Act One, creating a <u>break</u> in the <u>tension</u>.

2) <u>Footsteps</u> are often heard <u>offstage</u> — at the start of Act Four this <u>increases</u> the <u>tension</u>, as the audience doesn't know <u>who</u> is about to appear and <u>what effect</u> on the action they will have.

3) The <u>drumrolls</u> at the end of the play create a <u>harsh</u> mood. They also give a sense of <u>violence</u> and <u>finality</u> as Proctor dies.

Staging and Design

Directors and designers have to decide <u>which</u> moods they want to <u>highlight</u> in a production. They then have to work out exactly <u>how</u> to do this — see <u>Section Four</u> for more about staging and design.

Don't go to the theatre in space — there's no atmosphere...

REVISION TASK

Choose a key moment from 'The Crucible' not mentioned on this page and write a paragraph about a mood you would emphasise if you were staging this part of the play. Answer the following questions:

1) Why do you want to bring out this mood?
2) How would you emphasise this particular mood?
3) What would the effect of this mood be on the audience?

Tick list:
✓ one key mood
✓ specific examples of how mood is created
✓ effect on audience

Stage Directions

A playwright's stage directions are a bit like my dad during a family photo — they tell everyone where to stand, who to look at and when to smile. Apart from there isn't really much smiling in this play...

Miller uses different styles of stage directions in 'The Crucible'

1) Miller provides lots of stage directions for *The Crucible* — many of them are very detailed. They include instructions for speech, movement, gestures, facial expressions, costumes, lighting, sound and set design.

2) He also includes long, detailed notes about individual characters and their stories (see p.23).

3) Some of the stage directions are straightforward and instruct performers on how to do something. For example, the stage directions at the end of Act Three say that Hale "*slams the door*" as he exits the room.

4) Other stage directions are more poetic and descriptive, giving performers ideas about how to communicate meaning to the audience — when Proctor enters the prison cell in Act Four, the stage directions describe his eyes as "*misty, as though webs had overgrown them.*" A performer could show this through exaggerated blinking, or by presenting a vacant expression.

The start of each act has detailed stage directions

See p.20 for more on stage directions about lighting and set design.

1) Each act has a new setting, and Miller includes detailed notes about how these should look on stage.

2) He gives specific ideas about how each setting should appear to the audience and what messages it should communicate.

3) There are clear instructions about set design — at the start of Act Four, the stage directions state that the cell should be "*in darkness but for the moonlight*" and have "*a great, heavy door*" and "*a high barred window*". Following these instructions could create a sombre, dark mood for the act.

4) Naturalistic lighting is particularly important to Miller. At the start of Act Three, he instructs that there should be "*sunlight pouring through two high windows*". This brightness could reflect the imposing atmosphere of the court.

This 2014 production created the morning sunlight Miller refers to in Act One.

© Donald Cooper/photostage

Stage directions give performers key information

Stage directions guide the actors in how they should perform at a particular moment. Here are some examples of what information stage directions can reveal to a performer about their character:

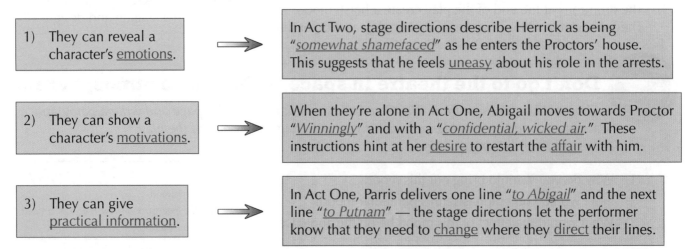

1) They can reveal a character's emotions.
→ In Act Two, stage directions describe Herrick as being "*somewhat shamefaced*" as he enters the Proctors' house. This suggests that he feels uneasy about his role in the arrests.

2) They can show a character's motivations.
→ When they're alone in Act One, Abigail moves towards Proctor "*Winningly*" and with a "*confidential, wicked air.*" These instructions hint at her desire to restart the affair with him.

3) They can give practical information.
→ In Act One, Parris delivers one line "*to Abigail*" and the next line "*to Putnam*" — the stage directions let the performer know that they need to change where they direct their lines.

Stage Directions

Stage directions add to subtexts in the play

1) The stage directions in *The Crucible* often reveal things that aren't explicitly expressed. This includes the underlying tensions between characters, their hidden motivations and their unspoken thoughts.

These subtexts link to wider ideas in the play about how Salem society was flawed — tensions and grievances were present, but couldn't publicly be expressed.

2) For example, Act Two begins with John and Elizabeth being polite and friendly to each other, but the stage directions note that "*a sense of their separation rises*", hinting at their marital problems.

Effect on the Audience

The audience never hear the stage directions — actors use them to shape their performances and give the audience a sense of the subtexts of their characters' dialogue.

3) In Act One, the stage directions say that Putnam is "*intent upon*" moving Parris "*toward the abyss*". This shows how his hidden motivation is to cause trouble for Parris, who he hates.

4) When Herrick vouches for Proctor in Act Three, Danforth's stage directions say that "*it is the reflection on himself he resents*". This reveals how Danforth's priority is protecting his reputation, not upholding justice as he outwardly suggests.

Miller includes detailed background notes

1) Miller gives introductory notes throughout Act One on the histories and motives of some important characters. The notes usually begin just after a character enters the stage.

2) The extra contextual information explains the personalities of characters, the story of the conflicts between characters, and characters' motivations.

3) For example, the notes on Thomas Putnam explain that his hostility towards others and his desire to take land from them comes from his anger that his brother-in-law wasn't given the role as Salem's minister.

4) Details like this aren't explained in the main play text, but they help actors to imagine how they might perform a particular role — it gives them deeper information about their characters.

5) There are also notes at the beginning of Act One which explain the history of Salem. They explore its problems with religion and authority, and also refer to the "*long-held hatreds of neighbours*" that are central to the play.

A director is faced with a dilemma about whether or not these notes should be read out. They add interesting information, but having a narrator would break with Miller's intended naturalistic style.

The background notes on Reverend Hale discuss how he sees himself as highly intelligent.

REVISION TASK

Which way to the stage? Down the corridor, second left...

Choose a stage direction from anywhere in the play that gives information about how an actor should deliver a particular line of speech. Write a paragraph about how you would interpret this stage direction in a performance. Make sure you cover:

1) The vocal skills you would use to deliver the line.
2) Any physical skills you would use at the same time.
3) How these skills get the message of the stage direction across to the audience.

Tick list:
✓ vocal skills
✓ physical skills
✓ audience response

Speech and Language

Performers don't just have to walk the walk, they have to talk the talk too. How they say things is just as important as what they say when it comes to communicating Miller's message to the audience.

Miller uses old-fashioned language to reflect the play's setting

1) Miller wanted to create a <u>realistic</u> portrayal of <u>17th-century Salem</u>, but he still needed characters to be <u>understood</u> by the audience.

2) He created his own form of speech, using <u>old-fashioned</u> words and phrases such as "<u>aye</u>" and "<u>goody</u>" (a contraction of 'good wife'), whilst still making sure that an audience in <u>20th-century America</u> would be able to <u>understand</u> what was being said.

3) He also sometimes uses old-fashioned <u>grammar</u>, e.g. "Then let you not earn it" to <u>imitate</u> how people might have spoken to each other 300 years ago.

> **Effect on the Audience**
>
> This kind of <u>language</u> informs the audience they're watching a play set in a <u>different era</u>, without making them feel <u>put off</u> or <u>distanced</u> from the action.

> **Vocal Skills — Accents**
>
> Miller <u>doesn't specify</u> the <u>accent</u> actors should use, so a director can <u>choose</u>. People from Salem <u>wouldn't</u> have had American accents — their accents would've been <u>similar</u> to the English <u>West Country</u> accent.

A character's speech can show their status...

1) The <u>less-educated</u> characters have more <u>non-standard</u> speech patterns. For example:

   - they use <u>double negatives</u>, e.g. Tituba says, "I <u>don't</u> compact with <u>no</u> Devil"
   - they drop the <u>final 'g'</u> in words such as "<u>searchin'</u>" and "<u>whippin'</u>"
   - they use <u>coarse language</u> — Proctor tells the court they are "raising up a <u>whore</u>"

2) This kind of speech makes the characters more <u>believable</u> and <u>realistic</u>.

3) In contrast, <u>well-educated</u> characters like Danforth and Hale often use <u>hyperbole</u> ("I should hang ten thousand that dared to rise against the law") and <u>Latin</u> language ("In nomine Domini Sabaoth...") which shows off their <u>education</u> and <u>status</u>.

> *Hyperbole is a technique where something is deliberately exaggerated for dramatic effect.*

... and it can reveal their personality

1) Proctor is very <u>direct</u> in his speech — he calls Abigail a "<u>whore</u>", and says "I may <u>speak my heart</u>" when he believes it's the right thing to do. This presents him as a <u>straightforward</u>, <u>blunt</u> character.

2) Abigail <u>adapts</u> her language which shows how <u>manipulative</u> she is. She <u>flirts</u> with John, <u>threatens</u> the girls, and speaks <u>confidently</u> at the trial. A performer playing Abigail might want to use different <u>tones of voice</u> to highlight how her <u>language changes</u> with different characters.

3) As well as showing his status, Danforth's <u>hyperbole</u> and <u>long speeches</u> show his sense of <u>self-importance</u> and his <u>pompous nature</u>.

> **Context**
>
> Speech could also be used to highlight the play's <u>political context</u>. In a <u>non-naturalistic production</u>, the actor playing Proctor could speak <u>directly</u> to the <u>audience</u> during his powerful "Because it is my name!" speech in Act Four. This might make them consider Miller's <u>wider message</u> about <u>persecution</u> in 1950s America.

© Drew Farrell/Royal Lyceum Theatre

This actor playing Proctor uses an expressive gesture, which supports Proctor's direct manner.

Speech and Language

The form of *The Crucible* is a play, meaning that it relies on speech between characters to tell its story.

Relationships can be shown through speech

1) Miller uses different kinds of <u>speech</u> to show how his characters <u>interact</u>:

- **DIALOGUE** is the <u>general term</u> for <u>speech</u> between characters <u>on stage</u>.
- A **DUOLOGUE** is when <u>two characters</u> have a <u>conversation</u> together.
- A **MONOLOGUE** is when a character makes a <u>speech</u> to <u>another character</u> or the <u>audience</u>.
- **CHORAL SPEECH** is when several characters say the <u>same thing</u> at the <u>same time</u>.

2) In Act One, there's lots of <u>fast-paced dialogue</u> as characters <u>question</u> and <u>accuse</u> each other. This reflects the <u>frantic atmosphere</u> in Salem and the <u>hostility</u> and <u>suspicion</u> between characters.

3) John and Elizabeth have a <u>duologue</u> at the start of Act Two when they're the only characters on stage. This creates an <u>intimate</u> atmosphere, focusing the audience on their troubled <u>relationship</u>.

4) Danforth has several <u>monologues</u> in Act Three, such as when he addresses the girls just after they enter the room. These long speeches show the attitude of <u>superiority</u> he displays towards others.

5) The girls use <u>choral speech</u> in Act Three. This shows that they are no longer <u>individuals</u> — they've become an obedient <u>mob</u>, responding to the <u>peer pressure</u> and <u>hysteria</u> that Abigail has started.

Miller uses poetic language and imagery

1) The <u>poetic language</u> and <u>imagery</u> in the play often show the <u>strength</u> and <u>depth</u> of a character's <u>emotions</u>. For example, Proctor uses a <u>metaphor</u> in Act Two when he tells Elizabeth that "an everlasting <u>funeral marches</u> round your heart", highlighting the depth of his <u>frustration</u> at her <u>coldness</u> towards him.

2) Lots of this imagery is <u>linked</u> to religion, which reminds the audience of its <u>importance</u> in the <u>Puritans' lives</u>.

3) Elizabeth uses a reference to a biblical story in a <u>simile</u> to describe the villagers' new <u>fear</u> and <u>respect</u> for Abigail — "the <u>crowd</u> will <u>part like the sea</u> for Israel". This could show her <u>anger</u>, <u>suspicion</u> or <u>jealousy</u>.

Vocal Skills

Performers need to understand the <u>meaning</u> behind the <u>imagery</u> their characters use so that they can get this across to the <u>audience</u>.

The play has a lot of hot and cold imagery

1) There are lots of references to <u>heat</u> and <u>hell</u> in *The Crucible*. For example, Danforth talks about the <u>trials</u> as being like "a <u>hot fire</u>" which "<u>melts</u> down all concealment". This links the <u>court</u> with <u>hell</u>, as it is traditionally depicted as a <u>hot</u>, <u>fiery</u> place.

2) <u>Passion</u> is also associated with <u>heat</u> — Abigail talks about John's "heat" that <u>draws her</u> to her window at night to see him.

3) <u>Elizabeth</u> is associated with <u>coldness</u> — she describes herself as a "<u>cold wife</u>" because she's <u>emotionally</u> cold towards Proctor.

4) Coldness is seen as <u>unnatural</u> and <u>wrong</u>. The girls talk about a "<u>cold wind</u>" in the court in Act Three when they first accuse Mary of <u>witchcraft</u>.

Costume is one way designers could engage with this imagery — e.g. in this 2006 production Abigail was dressed in red to reflect her passion.

The play's language? English, thankfully...

In the exam, you might need to write about how a performer should interpret their lines — e.g. Proctor's language is usually direct and blunt, so it'd be no good if the actor playing him spoke the lines softly.

Practice Questions

Time for you to show off your own technique — your question-answering technique that is. Have a go at this page of practice questions to check how much you've learnt about Miller's techniques in the play.

Quick Questions

1) Give one feature of the play that shows that it's a historical drama.

2) What is the effect of having an ordinary man as the tragic hero?

3) Which event is the resolution of the play?

4) How can you tell that Miller intended the play to be performed in a naturalistic style?
   Give three ways.

5) Give two examples from the play of stage directions that show a character's fear.

6) What is the effect of the sound of the drumrolls at the end of Act Four?

7) Give one piece of information about Salem that is revealed in the notes at the start of Act One.

8) What do Danforth's long speeches reveal about his character?

9) What is a duologue?

10) Why is there so much imagery related to heat in the play?

In-depth Questions

1) Describe one technique Miller uses to increase the tension on stage during Act Two, and explain how it adds to the tense atmosphere.

2) If you were directing a production of *The Crucible*, would you include Miller's background notes or not? Explain your answer.

3) The character notes about Reverend Hale say that he *"felt the pride of the specialist"* in being called to investigate the witchcraft in Salem. How might this information help an actor to portray that character?

4) Write a paragraph explaining the dramatic effect of the entrances and exits of different characters during Act One.

Practice Questions

Yep, you guessed it — the drama continues with even more questions. If you're feeling really eager, you could try writing your answers in exam conditions. Or you might prefer the 'tea-with-biscuit-in-hand' approach...

Exam-style Questions

> Read Act One from where Hale says "**Open yourself, Tituba**" to the end of the act, then answer Questions 1 and 2.

1) Imagine you're a sound designer working on the play. Explain how you would use sound to portray this extract effectively on stage for the audience. You should refer to atmosphere in your answer.

2) Imagine you're a director staging a production of *The Crucible*. Explain how a performer playing the character of Tituba might demonstrate her low status to the audience in this extract and elsewhere in the play. You should talk about performance skills, stage directions and use of stage space in your answer.

> Read from the start of Act Two to where Proctor says "**I think you're sad again. Are you?**", then answer Question 3 below.

3) Imagine you're a set designer working on *The Crucible*. Explain how you would use set design in this extract to create effects that reinforce the naturalistic style of the play.

> Find the part of Act Four where Proctor tears up his confession.
> Read from where Proctor says "**You will not use me!**" to where Elizabeth says "**He have his goodness now. God forbid I take it from him!**", then answer Questions 4 and 5 below.

4) John Proctor's tragic flaws are his pride and his desire to protect his reputation. Explain how a performer playing the character of Proctor might demonstrate his tragic flaws to the audience in this extract and elsewhere in the play.

5) Reread the last line of the extract, written in the box above. Imagine you're a performer playing Elizabeth. Describe how you would perform this line using your vocal and physical skills. You should explain the effects you want to create.

Character Performance — John Proctor

The Crucible contains a large cast of characters, but don't let that put you off. This section takes you through them one by one and offers lots of suggestions on how they might be performed. First up — John Proctor.

John Proctor is respected in Salem

1) John Proctor is the <u>head of his household</u> — he's <u>married</u> to Elizabeth Proctor and they have <u>three sons</u>.

2) He's a <u>respected farmer</u> in a Puritan society that values <u>hard work</u> (see p.6-7). This grants him <u>authority</u> in the eyes of certain characters — even Reverend Parris admits that he has "<u>great weight</u>" in the village.

> **John Proctor is...**
>
> **brave:** "I will fall like an ocean on that court!"
> **blunt:** "I like not the smell of this 'authority'."
> **guilt-ridden:** "I cannot mount the gibbet like a saint."

© Geraint Lewis / Alamy Stock Photo

3) However, Proctor's <u>influence</u> in the village has its <u>limits</u>. He's <u>aware</u> of the <u>higher status</u> and <u>authority</u> of Hale and Danforth, and he <u>can't stop</u> the accusations or the trials.

He's haunted by his mistakes

1) Proctor is the play's <u>tragic hero</u> (see p.18). His <u>proud nature</u> and <u>desire</u> to protect his <u>reputation</u> eventually cause his <u>downfall</u>.

2) He <u>hasn't</u> always been a <u>faithful</u> husband — seven months before the start of the play, he <u>committed adultery</u> with Abigail (see p.34-36). Elizabeth knows about his <u>infidelity</u> and has not <u>forgiven</u> him for it.

> Proctor's back story is a crucial part of his characterisation.

3) Proctor <u>regrets</u> committing adultery not only because he <u>betrayed</u> Elizabeth, but also because it's a <u>sin</u>. This sense of guilt <u>hangs over him</u> and affects the way he <u>behaves</u>. For example, his <u>anger</u> and <u>frustration</u> overwhelm him when he grabs Abigail "<u>by the hair</u>" for lying to the judges in Act Three.

4) His flaws make him a <u>complex</u> character — he isn't all good or all bad. This might be <u>challenging</u> for an actor to reflect <u>on stage</u>, but it makes him <u>more believable</u> and <u>easier</u> for the audience to <u>relate</u> to.

He's an opinionated character

1) Proctor is <u>cynical</u> about the <u>existence of witchcraft</u> and never believes Abigail's claims. This sets him apart as a <u>reasonable</u> character. Unlike other villagers, he doesn't use the <u>witch trials</u> for <u>personal gain</u>.

2) He's also <u>confident</u> and <u>unafraid</u> to <u>challenge authority</u>. This is shown in the way he <u>refuses</u> to hide his <u>dislike</u> for Reverend Parris — "I see no light of God in that man." However, Proctor's <u>outspoken</u> nature makes him <u>unpopular</u> with certain characters (e.g. Parris and Putnam) who are <u>glad</u> to see him <u>arrested</u>.

3) Overall, Proctor is presented as a <u>principled</u> man who stands by what he believes in. An actor could reflect this side to Proctor's character in performance:

> • Whenever Proctor expresses an opinion, an actor might <u>speak emphatically</u> to show <u>conviction</u>.
> • He could <u>stand tall</u> and take <u>centre stage</u> to add to the sense that he's <u>confident</u> in his <u>beliefs</u>.
> • In Act One, he might <u>shake his head</u> or <u>roll his eyes</u> while characters like Parris and Putnam are speaking — this would imply that Proctor isn't afraid to show when he <u>disagrees</u> with someone.

Character Performance — John Proctor

Proctor is a physically imposing character

1) The stage directions describe Proctor as "*in his prime*". An actor could reflect this in his performance:

- Proctor is in his mid-thirties, so he's younger than most of the other adults. This could be conveyed using energetic movements and gestures.
- As a farmer, Proctor spends a lot of time doing tough manual labour, so he's likely to have a muscular build. An actor could stick out his chest or draw back his shoulders to give the audience this impression.

2) Proctor's appearance changes in the three-month gap between Act Three and Act Four. An actor might use a hunched posture to show that he has lost his powerful build — this would attract sympathy from the audience.

He's in control of himself in Act One...

1) When Proctor is alone on stage with Abigail in Act One, there are signs that he's still attracted to her (e.g. "*a knowing smile*"), but he resists temptation and tells her to put their affair "out of mind".

2) Later in the act, Proctor demonstrates confidence when he challenges Parris and Putnam.

Act One — Physical Skills

- When Proctor is alone with Abigail, an actor might use closed body language, e.g. folded arms. This would suggest that he's remaining in control — he's determined not to back down.
- Later on, an actor might stand in an upright posture and hold eye contact with Parris to make Proctor seem self-assured.

Act One — Vocal Skills

- Proctor is committed to resisting Abigail's advances, so an actor might speak firmly, clearly and at a slow pace to show this.
- He might speak to Putnam in an authoritative tone ("We vote by name in this society, not by acreage"). This would add to the sense that he's a self-confident character.

... but he loses his composure during Act Two

1) Proctor tries to be affectionate with Elizabeth, but his affair means that their relationship is still troubled.

2) Hale's arrival catches Proctor off guard. He gets defensive under interrogation, before losing his temper when Elizabeth is arrested. An actor needs to use a range of skills to portray these contrasting emotions:

Act Two — Physical Skills

- An actor could smile warmly at Elizabeth to suggest that Proctor is trying to make her happy.
- In contrast, an unsettled facial expression would suggest that he's uncomfortable in Hale's presence.
- He might use frantic movements and gestures in his desperation to stop Elizabeth from being arrested.

Act Two — Vocal Skills

- Initially, an actor could use a casual tone to show Proctor's relaxed mood as he sits down for dinner.
- He might speak slowly and cautiously to Reverend Hale, as if Proctor is being careful of what he says.
- An actor could switch to a loud volume and a fast pace to express Proctor's anger at Elizabeth's arrest.

Character Performance — John Proctor

Proctor is powerless in Act Three...

1) In Act Three, Proctor is <u>desperate</u> to defend Elizabeth from Abigail's accusations of witchcraft — he tries to stay <u>composed</u> in front of the judges, but gets <u>frustrated</u> when they <u>won't listen</u> to him.

2) In the final section of the act, Proctor's desperation causes him to <u>lose all control</u> of his <u>emotions</u>.

Act Three — Physical Skills

- An actor may used <u>fixed eye contact</u> and <u>gentle gestures</u> when persuading Mary to <u>tell the truth</u>.
- However, he could use a <u>wide-eyed expression</u> or <u>erratic movements</u> to suggest that Proctor is concerned about losing control of the situation.
- An actor could emphasise Proctor's aggression and violence at the end of the act — he might <u>struggle wildly</u> when he's <u>accused</u> and <u>arrested</u>.

Act Three — Vocal Skills

- An actor may address the judges <u>slowly</u> and <u>gently</u>, as though Proctor is trying to appear <u>reasonable</u> ("I — I would free my wife, sir").
- He might use a <u>sarcastic</u> or <u>mocking tone</u> when Proctor realises they aren't listening.
- An actor could reflect Proctor's loss of control by <u>yelling aggressively</u> ("You are pulling Heaven down and raising up a whore!").

... but he finds strength in Act Four

1) In Act Four, Proctor has been in <u>prison</u> for <u>three months</u>. He hasn't seen Elizabeth in that period, so their reunion is an <u>intimate</u> moment — it's obvious to the audience that he still <u>loves</u> his wife.

2) Proctor is at <u>breaking point</u> after months of torture, and he can't decide whether or not to 'confess'. An actor's performance should convey Proctor's <u>emotional</u> and <u>physical anguish</u> to the audience.

Act Four — Physical Skills

- An actor may <u>move closer</u> to Elizabeth and <u>maintain eye contact</u> to show Proctor's <u>affection</u> for her.
- A <u>pained expression</u> and <u>laboured movements</u> could show Proctor's <u>discomfort</u> and emotional <u>turmoil</u>.
- When Proctor tears the confession, an actor may <u>stand taller</u> to give a sense of <u>decisiveness</u> and <u>pride</u>.

In this production, John sits close to Elizabeth in the final act.

© Donald Cooper/photostage

Act Four — Vocal Skills

- An actor may speak <u>slowly</u> and <u>quietly</u> to make Proctor's voice sound <u>heavy with emotion</u> — "What would you have me do?"
- Later in the act, Proctor seems to be <u>overcome</u> by the <u>weight</u> of these emotions. An actor's speech might become <u>quicker</u>, <u>louder</u> and <u>less clear</u> to suggest the <u>intensity</u> of his <u>feelings</u>.
- When Proctor finally makes up his mind, an actor may speak <u>firmly</u> to express <u>confidence</u> that he's made the <u>right decision</u>.

REVISION TASK

Proctor, Proctor — I feel like a... wait, wrong joke...

In a group, choose one person to be Proctor and sit them in the 'hot seat'. Then take turns to question them — the person in the 'hot seat' must remain in character. You might want to ask:

1) Why did Proctor have an affair with Abigail?
2) How does Proctor feel about Abigail now?
3) What are Proctor's thoughts and feelings about Elizabeth?

Imagine this interview is taking place at the start of Act One.

Character Performance — Elizabeth Proctor

Elizabeth is John's faithful wife. She appears as a cold character who keeps her emotions hidden. It's only really in the final act of the play that the audience sees a warmer, more emotional Elizabeth.

Elizabeth Proctor is a product of her time

© Donald Cooper/photostage

1) In many ways, Elizabeth Proctor is a typical Puritan <u>housewife</u> — she looks after the <u>household</u> and the <u>children</u> while her husband works on the <u>farm</u>.

2) She refers to herself as a "<u>covenanted Christian woman</u>", which means that she's a <u>faithful</u> Christian — according to Proctor, she's <u>never</u> even told a <u>lie</u>.

3) However, Elizabeth and Proctor don't go to <u>church</u> often and their third son <u>hasn't</u> been <u>baptised</u>. This is used as evidence that she's guilty of <u>witchcraft</u>.

4) As a woman, she has <u>no authority</u> in Salem. She has a <u>good reputation</u> like Proctor, but she's <u>powerless</u> to <u>defend herself</u> once she's <u>accused</u> by Abigail.

There's more about the context of the play in Section One.

Context — Women in Puritan Society

Puritans believed in <u>male authority</u> — women were seen as <u>inferior</u> to men, so they weren't allowed to <u>run businesses</u> or <u>own property</u>. They were also thought to be <u>weaker</u> and <u>more vulnerable</u> to being influenced by the <u>Devil</u>.

She struggles to cope with Proctor's affair

1) When Elizabeth is introduced to the audience, she still hasn't come to terms with Proctor's <u>infidelity</u>. She <u>loves</u> him, but she's <u>cautious</u> about showing any <u>emotion</u> towards him as a result of his <u>betrayal</u>.

2) The affair has made Elizabeth <u>suspicious</u> of her husband. For example, she <u>confronts</u> him when he says that he was alone with Abigail ("Why, then, it is not as you told me.")

Elizabeth Proctor is...

moral: "I am a good woman, I know it."

jealous: "She thinks to take my place"

frosty: "Your justice would freeze beer!"

3) It's also made her <u>insecure</u>. Towards the end of the play, she even <u>blames herself</u> for Proctor's actions and admits that she pushed him away by being a "<u>cold wife</u>" to him.

4) However, Elizabeth remains <u>loyal</u> to Proctor and <u>stands by him</u> at key moments throughout the play.

She isn't as young or attractive as Abigail

The costume designer is also responsible for Elizabeth's appearance and its effect on the audience (see p.58-60).

1) Miller doesn't describe Elizabeth's appearance — it's up to the <u>director</u> to decide which features of her character they want to <u>emphasise</u> through her presentation on stage. This will have an impact on the audience's <u>perception</u> of her.

2) Elizabeth might be portrayed as a <u>plain-looking</u> character to provide a contrast with Abigail's "*strikingly beautiful*" appearance — this would also make Elizabeth appear <u>less attractive</u>.

- Elizabeth is likely to be in her <u>mid-thirties</u> like Proctor, but she's been <u>ill</u> before the start of the play. An actor could <u>move slowly</u> and <u>shakily</u> in order to seem <u>weak</u>.

- An actor might put on a <u>sour-faced expression</u> and <u>smile infrequently</u> with Proctor to make Elizabeth seem <u>cold</u> and <u>unemotional</u> in comparison to Abigail.

Effect on the Audience

Highlighting Elizabeth's <u>plain appearance</u> and <u>coldness</u> would give the audience a <u>clearer idea</u> of why Proctor had an <u>affair</u>, although it wouldn't make it <u>acceptable</u>.

Character Performance — Elizabeth Proctor

Elizabeth isn't seen on stage in Act One

1) An actor could use the <u>information</u> provided by <u>other characters</u> to inform their portrayal of Elizabeth.

2) For example, Reverend Parris mentions a <u>rumour</u> that Elizabeth hasn't been going to church in order to <u>avoid</u> Abigail. This strongly implies that Elizabeth <u>hates</u> Abigail and <u>blames</u> her for Proctor's affair.

3) Abigail describes Elizabeth as a "<u>cold</u>, <u>snivelling</u> woman". She's <u>exaggerating</u>, but it's significant that she mentions her <u>coldness</u> — this hints at the way Elizabeth might behave towards Proctor in <u>Act Two</u>.

She's cold towards Proctor in Act Two...

1) In Act Two, Elizabeth wants to come across as <u>calm</u> and <u>composed</u> to Proctor. However, this is just a <u>front</u> — she's actually trying to <u>hide</u> the fact that she's still <u>hurting</u> as a result of his affair with Abigail.

2) When Elizabeth is <u>arrested</u>, her <u>reaction</u> is <u>subdued</u>. She's <u>scared</u>, but goes away with Cheever <u>quietly</u>.

Act Two — Physical Skills

- <u>Proxemics</u> (see p.81) could show that Elizabeth is feeling hurt — the actor could <u>position</u> herself <u>far away</u> from Proctor on stage. She might also <u>flinch</u> when he "<u>kisses</u>" her.
- She may <u>stare</u> at Proctor with a <u>narrow gaze</u> when he mentions Abigail, as if she's trying to decide whether or not he's being <u>honest</u>.
- When Elizabeth is arrested, an actor could <u>bow her head</u> to show that she's <u>resigned</u> to her <u>fate</u>.

Act Two — Vocal Skills

- The stage directions say that Elizabeth speaks "<u>very coldly</u>" to Proctor. An actor could use <u>minimal intonation</u> or an <u>unaffectionate tone</u>.
- She might <u>raise her voice</u> at times, as though she struggles to hide her <u>bitterness</u> and <u>anger</u> ("I will be your only wife, or no wife at all!")
- Later on, her voice might <u>tremble</u> to express <u>fear</u> and <u>uncertainty</u> about what is going to happen to her ("I think I must go with them.")

... but she tries to defend him in Act Three

1) Elizabeth only makes a <u>brief appearance</u> in Act Three — she's asked to confirm or deny Proctor's claim that he had an affair with Abigail.

2) She's <u>uncomfortable</u> with Danforth's <u>scrutiny</u>. She senses that her response is <u>important</u>, and she's <u>desperate</u> to protect her husband.

3) Earlier in the play, Elizabeth describes herself as a "<u>good woman</u>". Being <u>under pressure</u> to lie puts her in a difficult <u>moral</u> position.

4) An actor could show her <u>discomfort</u> to the audience:

© Drew Farrell/Royal Lyceum Theatre

Act Three — Physical Skills

- Elizabeth is <u>under pressure</u> from Danforth, so an actor's <u>body language</u> might be <u>tense</u> or <u>uneasy</u>.
- She may look around the room or <u>avoid eye contact</u> with Danforth to put off answering his questions.
- An actor could <u>wring her hands together</u> whilst lying to suggest that it's <u>difficult</u> for Elizabeth to do.

Act Three — Vocal Skills

- An actor could use <u>long pauses</u> and <u>hesitations</u> to suggest that Elizabeth is <u>unsure</u> of how to respond.
- Elizabeth isn't used to lying, so an actor's voice might <u>falter</u> when she denies that Proctor had an affair.
- Her speech may become <u>louder</u> and <u>high-pitched</u> when she realises the <u>consequences</u> of her answer — "Oh, God!" This would suggest that Elizabeth <u>fears</u> for Proctor's welfare now, as well as her own.

Section Three — Character and Performance

Character Performance — Elizabeth Proctor

Elizabeth has mixed emotions in Act Four

1) In Act Four, Elizabeth is more <u>open</u> and <u>sincere</u> with Proctor than she was in <u>Act Two</u> — she hasn't <u>forgotten</u> about Proctor's affair, but she appears to be more willing to <u>forgive</u> him for it than before.

2) Elizabeth doesn't want her husband to <u>die</u>, but knows that it's a <u>sin</u> to make a <u>false confession</u>. She's <u>determined</u> to support Proctor, but she's <u>conflicted</u> about his decision to <u>sacrifice himself</u>.

© Donald Cooper/photostage

Here, the actor's body language is direct — she turns her body to face Proctor.

Act Four — Physical Skills

- An actor could use <u>open body language</u> with Proctor and <u>position</u> herself more <u>closely</u> to him than she has done in previous acts. This would suggest that Elizabeth wants to show him more <u>warmth</u> and <u>affection</u> than before.

- She might also use <u>reassuring gestures</u> to comfort Proctor, like pulling him closer to her or resting her hand softly on his arm.

- Elizabeth wants to stay strong, but it's hard for her — when Hathorne asks Proctor for his <u>plea</u>, she starts *"weeping"*. An actor could adopt a <u>collapsed posture</u> to reinforce the idea that her <u>composure</u> has finally <u>broken</u>.

Act Four — Vocal Skills

- An actor could use a <u>gentle tone</u> to show that Elizabeth isn't as <u>bitter</u> about the affair as she used to be.
- She might speak <u>without hesitation</u>, as though she <u>isn't hiding</u> her <u>true thoughts</u> and <u>feelings</u> anymore.
- When Proctor is taken away, an actor might <u>cry out</u> to show that Elizabeth is no longer <u>containing</u> her <u>emotions</u>. She may include several <u>sobbing pauses</u> during the last line ("He have his goodness now.")

In the exam, link performance suggestions to the text

The <u>sample answer</u> below shows you how you might <u>write</u> about performing <u>Elizabeth</u> on stage:

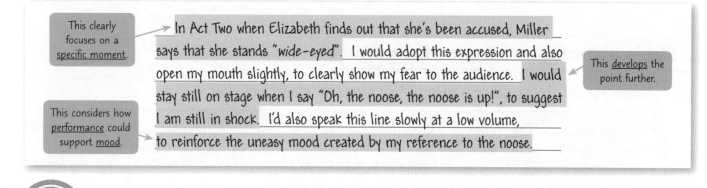

This clearly focuses on a <u>specific moment</u>.

In Act Two when Elizabeth finds out that she's been accused, Miller says that she stands "wide-eyed". I would adopt this expression and also open my mouth slightly, to clearly show my fear to the audience. I would stay still on stage when I say "Oh, the noose, the noose is up!", to suggest I am still in shock. I'd also speak this line slowly at a low volume, to reinforce the uneasy mood created by my reference to the noose.

This <u>develops</u> the point further.

This considers how <u>performance</u> could support <u>mood</u>.

REVISION TASK

Oh, Elizabeth — of all the times to start telling porkies...

Improvise an imaginary scene in which Elizabeth sacks Abigail. You will be performing the role of Elizabeth, so you'll need a partner to play Abigail. Your performance should do the following:

1) Explore Elizabeth's reasons for sacking Abigail.
2) Use a combination of physical and vocal skills.
3) Include an aside in which Elizabeth shares her inner thoughts and feelings with the audience.

Tick list:
✓ character's backstory
✓ appropriate physical and vocal performance skills
✓ audience interaction

Character Performance — Abigail Williams

Abigail Williams is a nasty piece of work — she's got the hots for Proctor and won't take 'no' for an answer. Oh, and not to mention that she accuses just about the whole village of witchcraft...

Abigail Williams is the villain of the play

© Geraint Lewis / Alamy Stock Photo

1) Abigail Williams is a <u>seventeen-year-old</u> who lives with her <u>uncle</u>, Reverend Parris (see p.37). She's the <u>main antagonist</u> in the play — she causes <u>pain</u> and <u>suffering</u> for other characters.

> **Abigail Williams is...**
>
> **dishonest:** "It is a wonder they do believe her."
> **intimidating:** "I'll beat you, Betty!"
> **heartless:** "She thinks to dance with me on my wife's grave!"

2) In the stage directions, Miller says that Abigail has an "*endless capacity for dissembling*" — in other words, she's skilled at <u>manipulating</u> other characters by <u>lying</u> and <u>hiding her true nature</u> from them.

3) She tries to convince other characters that she's <u>innocent</u>, but she's actually <u>disobedient</u> and doesn't follow Salem's <u>strict rules</u>. For example, she's been punished in the past for "<u>laughter during prayer</u>".

4) Abigail uses the trials to pursue her own <u>selfish</u> goals — she wants to be with Proctor, so she <u>accuses</u> Elizabeth. Abigail accuses the <u>other villagers</u> because they've been <u>spreading rumours</u> about her.

She's had a troubled upbringing

1) Abigail's parents were <u>brutally murdered</u> by "Indians" when she was a young girl — she even saw it happen. This might help to explain why her own behaviour is so <u>vengeful</u> and <u>unforgiving</u>.

> During the 17th century, the Puritan settlers in Salem often lived in fear of Native American raids.

2) She was raised by Parris, who has "*no interest in children*". This suggests that it was a <u>harsh upbringing</u>.

3) More recently, Abigail worked as the Proctors' <u>housekeeper</u> — this is how her relationship with Proctor <u>began</u>. Elizabeth found out and <u>dismissed</u> Abigail, which is another reason why Abigail wants <u>revenge</u>.

She's a young and beautiful girl

1) Abigail's <u>physical appearance</u> is an important part of her <u>characterisation</u>:

- At <u>seventeen</u>, Abigail is one of the <u>youngest</u> characters in the play. A director would probably cast a young actor, but her youthfulness could be emphasised using <u>swift</u> and <u>energetic movements</u>.
- Miller doesn't describe Abigail's <u>height</u> or <u>build</u>, but an actor could use an <u>upright posture</u> to seem <u>taller</u> than the other girls. This would highlight her <u>authority</u> and single her out as their <u>ringleader</u>.
- She's described as "*strikingly beautiful*" — to reflect this in performance, an actor might speak and move with <u>confidence</u>. This would show that she's <u>aware</u> of her <u>beauty</u> and the <u>power</u> it gives her.

2) Abigail uses her physical appearance to <u>influence</u> and <u>deceive</u> other characters. She knows that Proctor is <u>attracted</u> to her, and she convinces the judges that she is a <u>harmless teenager</u>.

> **Effect on the Audience**
>
> Abigail's <u>youthful appearance</u> might even deceive the <u>audience</u> at the start — if only for a <u>short time</u>. This would make it more <u>surprising</u> when it becomes clear that she's an <u>evil</u> and <u>destructive character</u>.

Character Performance — Abigail Williams

Abigail is manipulative in Act One...

1) Throughout Act One, Abigail tries to appear <u>innocent</u> to Parris, Hale and the other villagers. She <u>plays down</u> the <u>seriousness</u> of her own actions, before claiming that she was the <u>victim</u> of witchcraft <u>herself</u>.

2) Abigail only reveals her <u>true nature</u> when she's <u>alone</u> with the other girls or Proctor. For example, she <u>bullies</u> the girls into keeping quiet about what happened in the woods, then <u>flirts openly</u> with Proctor.

3) An actor has to use a range of physical and vocal skills to reflect these <u>changes</u> in Abigail's <u>behaviour</u>:

Act One — Physical Skills

- Abigail pretends she was only dancing in the forest, so an actor may <u>shake her head</u> and use an <u>open-mouthed expression</u> to express <u>shock</u> when Parris asks if she performed <u>witchcraft</u>.
- When Abigail is alone with the girls, an actor could use <u>authoritative body language</u> and a <u>central stage position</u> to suggest to the audience that she's the <u>dominant figure</u>.
- An actor could show Abigail's feelings for Proctor by using <u>persistent eye contact</u> and keeping <u>near him</u> on stage. An actor might also use <u>physical contact</u> to show her passion for him.

Act One — Vocal Skills

- An actor could speak <u>softly</u> and at a <u>higher pitch</u> when Parris and Hale are present to highlight Abigail's young age and make her seem too <u>innocent</u> to commit a <u>serious crime</u> like <u>witchcraft</u>.
- In contrast, she might use a slightly <u>lower pitch</u> around Proctor to appear more <u>mature</u>.
- To <u>intimidate</u> the other girls, she might speak <u>slowly</u> and in a <u>menacing tone</u> — "I will bring a pointy reckoning that will shudder you". This would make her sound <u>serious</u> and <u>threatening</u>.

... and not much changes in Act Three

Abigail doesn't appear on stage in Act Two, but her actions offstage lead to Elizabeth's arrest.

1) In Act Three, Abigail wants to persuade the judges that she's <u>telling the truth</u> and Mary Warren is <u>lying</u>. She doesn't seem to be <u>intimidated</u> by their authority, and she even stands up to Danforth at one point.

2) The judges still don't know who to believe, so Abigail tries a <u>different approach</u>. She pretends to have <u>visions</u> of a "<u>yellow bird</u>" and accuses Mary of sending it to <u>attack</u> her. The other girls follow her lead.

© Donald Cooper/photostage

Act Three — Physical Skills

- An actor may use a <u>serious expression</u> whilst <u>maintaining eye contact</u> with the judges to appear <u>convincing</u>. She might also <u>remain still</u> to reflect that Abigail is a <u>calm</u> and <u>collected</u> liar.
- When Mary cracks and accuses Proctor, Abigail "<u>reaches out</u>" to <u>comfort</u> her. An actor might <u>smile mockingly</u> at Proctor at the same time to suggest that Abigail knows his fate is <u>sealed</u>.

Act Three — Vocal Skills

- An actor could use <u>inflection</u> (see p.80) to make Abigail's denial of the affair seem <u>convincing</u>. When she says "Mr Danforth, he is lying!", including lots of <u>variation</u> in the <u>pitch</u> and <u>tone</u> of her <u>voice</u> to <u>emphasise</u> certain words would help to make Abigail's defence appear <u>passionate</u> and <u>heartfelt</u>.
- An actor could speak at a <u>steady volume</u> and <u>pace</u> to show that Abigail is <u>self-assured</u>. However, she may <u>raise her voice</u> in <u>anger</u> at Danforth for questioning her honesty — "I'll not have such looks!"
- To express Abigail's 'fear' of the 'bird', an actor could use a change in <u>pitch</u>. For example, her voice might <u>steadily increase</u> in pitch during the action until it reaches a <u>piercing shriek</u>.

Character Performance — Abigail Williams

Abigail can be performed in several ways

© Donald Cooper/photostage

1) The most common interpretation of Abigail's character is that she's inherently evil. In Act Four, Parris reveals that she has stolen from him and run away, which seems to confirm her cruelty.

2) During the play, an actor might suggest Abigail enjoys condemning people with false accusations of witchcraft to highlight her evilness.

Effect on the Audience

This interpretation of Abigail would make an audience even less sympathetic towards her character. They're unlikely to forgive any of her actions if an actor's performance shows no conscience or remorse.

3) However, Abigail's back story (see p.34) could allow her to be portrayed more sympathetically at times:

- In Act One, an actor's voice might tremble slightly when Abigail tells Parris that she loves Betty. This would suggest that she's afraid that another member of her family might die.

- An actor may highlight her vulnerability by crying or clinging to Proctor when he rejects her. This would make her feelings seem genuine, or imply that she was used and then cast aside by him.

Effect on the Audience

This interpretation might attract more sympathy for Abigail, but it wouldn't justify her actions — it'd be a way of adding depth and complexity to the character.

4) The audience might also understand that Abigail is a teenage girl in a society that represses women — especially unmarried ones. An actor may present her behaviour as the result of boredom or frustration.

Use specific details to write about character performance

Take a look at the sample answer below — it shows how you could write about performing Abigail on stage:

> This makes a clear point and explains its effect on the audience.

When Proctor enters in Act One, the stage directions say that Abigail stands "on tiptoe". Here, I would bounce up and down slightly to show that I am excited and want his attention. I would move to within inches of Proctor and say "I'd almost forgot how strong you are" in a breathless voice, as this use of proxemics and vocal delivery would show my intense desire for him. Finally, I would use this limited space to put both hands suggestively on Proctor's chest. I would look comfortable in this position to reflect how close I have been to Proctor in the past.

> This develops the point further.

> This demonstrates good knowledge of Abigail's backstory.

REVISION TASK

WANTED — a housekeeper who isn't a total nightmare...

Read Act Three from "I believe him!" to "Oh please, Mary! Don't come down." Write a couple of paragraphs about how you would perform Abigail here. Your interpretation should mention:

1) Her body language and use of space on stage.
2) Her voice (e.g. pitch, tone, volume, timing).
3) The effects of these choices on the audience.

> Remember — an interpretation is personal. You can interpret the character however you like, as long as you're able to support your ideas.

Section Three — Character and Performance

Character Performance — Reverend Parris

Reverend Parris only thinks of himself — not exactly the type of behaviour you'd expect from a man of God.

Reverend Parris always feels victimised

1) Parris is in his <u>mid-forties</u>. He used to be a <u>merchant</u>, but he's been the <u>minister</u> in Salem for <u>three years</u>.

2) Miller says that there's "<u>*little good* to be said for him</u>", so an actor may highlight his <u>negative qualities</u> — for example, he's a <u>suspicious</u> man who believes that the villagers are trying to "drive" him out of Salem.

3) He feels that he's <u>undervalued</u> and <u>underpaid</u> for his role as the minister of Salem, claiming that "I am not used to this <u>poverty</u>".

4) Parris is also <u>selfish</u> — he doesn't care about his parishioners and he's concerned that Betty's 'illness' will make him <u>look bad</u>.

Parris prays beside Betty's bed.

© Drew Farrell/Royal Lyceum Theatre

> **Reverend Parris is...**
>
> **disliked**: "Abigail, do you understand that I have many enemies?"
> **greedy**: "he preach nothin' but golden candlesticks"
> **self-centred**: "You cannot hang this sort. There is danger for me."

He's a self-interested character

1) In Act One, it's <u>obvious</u> that Parris only cares about <u>himself</u>. This could be shown in different ways:

> • An actor could use <u>exaggerated movements</u> to draw the audience's attention to him, rather than Betty. He might <u>barely look</u> at Betty to suggest that he's <u>more worried</u> about his <u>reputation</u> than his <u>daughter</u>.
> • Parris "<u>*rushes to embrace*</u>" Betty when she <u>wakes up</u> and <u>accuses</u> other villagers of witchcraft, but an actor might <u>move away</u> from her just as quickly to shout the "<u>*prayer of thanksgiving*</u>". This would add to the audience's impression that Parris's main concern was always about <u>securing his reputation</u>.

2) In Act Three, an actor might encourage the judges by <u>nodding excitedly</u> at them or speaking with a <u>rising intonation</u>. This would suggest that Parris believes the trials could work to his <u>advantage</u>.

He's ruined at the end of the play

1) In Act Four, Parris continues to act <u>selfishly</u>. He <u>pleads</u> with Danforth to <u>postpone</u> the <u>executions</u> as he's <u>worried</u> he'll get caught up in a "<u>riot</u>". An actor might express these concerns in a <u>nervous tone</u>.

2) An actor may <u>tremble with fear</u> and use a <u>stuttering</u>, <u>choked voice</u> when Parris tells Danforth that someone planted a dagger in his door. This would show the audience that Parris <u>fears for his life</u>.

3) When Parris reveals that he's "<u>penniless</u>", an actor could follow the stage directions by <u>sobbing</u> into their hands. This would show that Parris feels <u>humiliated</u>.

I'm starting to think Parris is ready for a career change...

Choose a moment from the play involving Parris. In a group, reenact this moment without using words. You could use the following techniques to communicate details about Parris's character:

1) Facial expressions and eye contact.
2) Gestures and body language.
3) The use of proxemics to convey relationships on stage.

> If you're on your own, you can just write a couple of paragraphs about which physical skills you would use at this moment instead.

Character Performance — Reverend Hale

Reverend Hale's character changes over the course of the play — make sure you understand how and why.

Hale is devoted to restoring order in Salem

1) Hale is a <u>witchcraft expert</u> who is summoned to Salem by Parris.

2) He's <u>deeply religious</u>. The stage directions say that *"His goal is light, goodness and its preservation"*, so an actor might choose to portray him as a <u>moral</u> man who wants to do the <u>right thing</u>.

3) However, he thinks that he's just as <u>clever</u> as *"philosophers"* or *"scientists"* — an actor may interpret this as a sign of <u>arrogance</u>.

4) At the start of the play, Hale is <u>blinded</u> by his faith — he's easily swept up by the <u>hysteria</u> and assumes that the girls' accusations are <u>true</u>. He finally realises that they were <u>lying</u>, but it's <u>too late</u>.

> **Reverend Hale is...**
>
> **fair:** "What I have heard in her favour, I will not fear to testify"
>
> **compassionate:** "I would save your husband's life"
>
> **guilt-stricken:** "There is blood on my head!"

He's confident and purposeful in Act One...

1) Hale is <u>full of confidence</u> in Act One. This might be shown using <u>strong body language</u> — an actor could stand in an <u>upright posture</u> with his <u>hands on his hips</u>. He could also put on a <u>serious expression</u> to suggest that Hale is <u>determined</u> to rid Salem of witchcraft.

2) An actor playing Hale may <u>position</u> himself <u>close</u> to other characters and use <u>unwavering eye contact</u> with them to show that he's <u>focused</u> on uncovering the truth about the girls' behaviour.

3) He could use a <u>self-assured tone</u> and speak at a <u>regular pace</u> whenever Hale is talking about witchcraft — this would suggest that he's a <u>knowledgeable</u>, <u>intelligent</u> character.

4) An actor might also use vocal skills to reflect Hale's <u>compassionate</u> side. For example, he might use a <u>gentler tone</u> and a <u>quieter volume</u> when he's speaking to Rebecca Nurse.

... but he slowly starts to regret getting involved

1) In Act Two, Hale is <u>concerned</u> when he hears about Rebecca Nurse's <u>arrest</u>. Although he <u>reassures</u> Francis Nurse that she'll be found innocent, the stage directions say that he's *"deeply troubled"*. An actor might <u>frown</u> or <u>run a hand</u> worriedly through his <u>hair</u> to show how the news has <u>disturbed</u> him.

2) By Act Three, Hale is worried that the trials are going <u>too far</u> — an actor might reflect this by <u>increasing the space</u> between Hale and the judges. This would suggest that he wants to <u>distance himself</u> from the <u>injustice</u> of the court.

3) An actor's vocal delivery might get steadily <u>louder</u>, <u>stronger</u> and <u>more agitated</u> to highlight Hale's <u>growing frustration</u> that <u>innocent</u> people are being <u>accused</u>.

4) Hale becomes so <u>exasperated</u> by the trials that he storms out of the courtroom and *"slams the door"*. At this moment, an actor might use a <u>furious expression</u> or even <u>throw</u> his books to the floor in order to emphasise Hale's <u>extreme anger</u>.

5) By Act Four, Hale's character has <u>completely changed</u>. He feels guilty about his role in the trials, so an actor's voice may become <u>increasingly desperate</u> — he may speak in a <u>pleading tone</u> and at an <u>increased pace and volume</u>, or <u>choke on his words</u>. This would present a <u>contrast</u> to Hale's <u>confidence</u> in Act One.

© Donald Cooper/photostage

EXAM TIP

Hale takes a while to get his head out of the clouds...

Hale is one of many characters who change throughout the play. In your exam, you could suggest how an actor could use physical and vocal skills to present his character arc convincingly on stage.

Character Performance — Danforth

Danforth has the difficult task of keeping order and finding witches in Salem — unfortunately, he fails at both.

Danforth is the Salem's most powerful figure

© Drew Farrell/Royal Lyceum Theatre

1) Deputy-Governor Danforth is the <u>judge</u> who <u>oversees</u> the <u>witch trials</u>.

2) He's aware of his <u>high status</u> in Salem, and his self-importance often makes him seem <u>arrogant</u>. In Act Three, an actor may show this by asking Mary "Do you know who I am?" while <u>looking down</u> at her <u>crossly</u>.

3) He believes that he's <u>fair</u>, but often he <u>isn't</u> — he <u>accepts</u> the girls' claims and <u>ignores</u> Proctor when he brings evidence that they're <u>making it up</u>.

4) He cares more about his <u>reputation</u> than <u>justice</u> — he only goes ahead with the executions in Act Four so that he isn't accused of "<u>floundering</u>".

He's authoritative but gullible in Act Three

1) In Act Three, an actor could convey Danforth's authority by <u>drawing back</u> their shoulders into an <u>upright posture</u>. This would make him appear <u>taller</u> and <u>more imposing</u>, particularly if he stands <u>centre stage</u>.

2) Danforth is in his <u>sixties</u>, but he may speak <u>loudly</u> and <u>animatedly</u> to assert his authority. An actor may interrupt others in a <u>superior tone</u> to show that Danforth thinks he's <u>more knowledgeable</u> than them.

3) An actor's vocal delivery could become <u>louder</u> and <u>more forceful</u> when Danforth asks Elizabeth "Answer my question! Is your husband a lecher!" He might also <u>slam his hands down</u> on the table to show that Danforth is becoming increasingly <u>angry</u> and <u>impatient</u> with Elizabeth's <u>indecision</u>.

Danforth is...

narrow-minded: "But proof, sir, proof."
insulting: "You are a foolish old man."
ruthless: "Hang them high over the town!"

4) Danforth is <u>biased</u> towards the <u>girls</u> throughout Act Three. An actor might <u>maintain eye contact</u> with the girls and <u>nod</u> whilst they're speaking to suggest that he's a <u>gullible</u> character who is taken in by their <u>lies</u>.

He doesn't admit to his mistakes in Act Four

1) In Act Four, Parris tells Danforth that Abigail has run away. At this moment, Danforth <u>realises</u> that he has been <u>deceived</u> by the girls, so an actor might put on a <u>wide-eyed facial expression</u> to reflect his <u>surprise</u>.

2) Danforth is angry with <u>himself</u> for believing the girls, but he takes it out on <u>Parris</u> — when he calls Parris a "brainless man", an actor could <u>grit his teeth</u> and use <u>violent gestures</u> to express Danforth's <u>frustration</u>.

3) Danforth is "<u>*deeply worried*</u>", but he regains his composure and decides to proceed with the executions. At this point, an actor may take a <u>deep breath</u> and <u>stand taller</u> to highlight his determination to carry on.

4) Later in Act Four, Danforth seems <u>cold</u> and <u>unemotional</u> when he sends Proctor to be <u>hanged</u>. An actor might use a <u>blank expression</u> as Proctor is led away to show that Danforth is <u>unaffected</u> by this <u>decision</u>.

Effect on the Audience

Danforth has the <u>final say</u> in the trials, so the audience is likely to see him as <u>selfish</u> and <u>hypocritical</u> in Act Four — he knows that he should <u>postpone</u> the executions, but goes through with them to <u>save face</u>.

EXAM TIP

Danforth? I wonder what happened to the first three...

The use of proxemics and levels can have a powerful effect on the audience, so they're definitely worth bearing in mind. They reveal more about onstage relationships and the status of individual characters.

Character Performance — The Victims

All in all, nineteen people were hanged during the real Salem witch trials. Miller doesn't have time to cover them all, so he focuses on a few of them to show just how cruel and unnecessary these executions were.

Tituba is an outsider

1) Tituba is Parris's slave. She helps the girls make charms and potions in the woods, and is one of the first villagers to be accused of witchcraft.

2) Parris brought Tituba from Barbados, so she's a racial and cultural outsider in Salem. An actor could highlight this by using a different accent.

Character Performance — Tituba

- In Act One, an actor might cover her face with her hands or use a hunched posture to suggest that Tituba is frightened by Abigail's accusation.

- In Act Four, Tituba is delusional — an actor may rock back and forth and mutter at a quick pace to show the audience that she has lost her mind.

Giles Corey is brave but argumentative

1) Giles Corey is Proctor's 83-year-old neighbour. His old age might be shown to the audience using a stooped posture and a slow gait.

2) He is a grumpy character in Act One, so an actor could scowl or shake his head disapprovingly when others are speaking.

3) He can be argumentative, which often gets him into trouble. An actor could show this by replying quickly to the other characters' lines — this would suggest that he doesn't think before he speaks.

4) In Act Three, Giles demonstrates bravery when he accuses Thomas Putnam of getting his daughter to lie in court. Here, an actor may stick out his chest to show that Giles isn't afraid to stand up to the judges, in spite of their higher status.

5) The audience hears about Giles's death in Act Four. He refused to enter a plea about witchcraft and died under torture — this shows his strength and integrity.

© Drew Farrell/Royal Lyceum Theatre

Giles is one of the only characters to create humour. His sarcasm and bluntness in Act Three defy the judges' authority and provide much-needed comic relief for the audience.

Rebecca Nurse is highly regarded in Salem

1) Rebecca Nurse is the elderly wife of Francis Nurse (see p.42). She is known throughout Salem for her kindness and gentleness. An actor may speak softly and show understanding with others to reflect this.

2) She's a level-headed character who sees through the girls' lies. An actor could show this by saying her lines in a thoughtful tone and maintaining an indifferent expression when other characters are shocked.

3) She shows courage by sticking to her principles throughout the play, even when she faces execution — in Act Four, an actor could use a defiant tone to show Rebecca's inner strength ("Let you fear nothing!")

And I thought Drama exams were a trial...

Find the moment at the end of Act One where Tituba confesses to witchcraft. Write a list of the physical and vocal skills you would use to play Tituba at this moment. You should think about:

1) Her reaction to Abigail's accusations.
2) How she interacts with Reverend Parris.
3) How she interacts with Reverend Hale.

Tick list:
✓ physical and vocal skills
✓ interaction between different characters

Character Performance — The Girls

The girls follow their ringleader, Abigail (see p.34-36), and their accusations wreak havoc in Salem. Actors playing the girls should stay close to one another and support each other to show they're strong as a group.

The girls are desperate to escape punishment

In Puritan society, dancing and other forms of entertainment were considered sinful (see p.6).

1) Parris comes across Abigail, Mercy Lewis, Betty and Mary in the <u>woods</u> before the start of Act One and sees some of them <u>dancing</u> — the girls are <u>worried</u> about the <u>consequences</u>, so they attempt to <u>shift the blame</u> onto other characters.

2) At first, the girls are <u>submissive</u> towards <u>male authority figures</u> — the <u>stage directions</u> suggest that Mercy and Mary are scared of Proctor. When he enters the room, the actors playing the girls may <u>avoid eye contact</u>, <u>bow their heads</u>, and <u>position</u> themselves <u>far away</u> from him to imply that they're <u>intimidated</u>.

3) Towards the end of Act One, Abigail realises that she can <u>escape punishment</u> by accusing <u>other people</u>. When Betty wakes up, she might <u>mimic</u> Abigail's behaviour to show that she's realised the <u>same thing</u>.

4) From this point onwards, the girls have more control over the other villagers than before. The actors' <u>body language</u> and <u>vocal delivery</u> might become <u>more confident</u> to show this important shift in <u>power</u>.

Mary Warren tries to do the honest thing...

1) Mary Warren is the Proctors' servant. She's <u>forced</u> by Proctor to testify against Abigail after Elizabeth is arrested. Proctor is <u>heavy-handed</u> with Mary, so an actor might <u>flinch</u> away from him when he's <u>close</u>.

2) In Act Three, Mary is <u>conflicted</u> — she feels <u>guilty</u> about lying to the judges and wants to tell the truth, but she's <u>terrified</u> of betraying the other girls. When Mary admits to Danforth that she lied in court, an actor might <u>keep her eyes to the floor</u> and <u>speak softly</u> to show that she feels <u>ashamed</u>, before <u>bursting into tears</u> to show that she's <u>overwhelmed</u> by the decision.

... but the other girls force her back into line

1) When Mary finally admits that she was <u>lying</u> in court, the other girls <u>work together</u> to prove her <u>wrong</u>. They know they're <u>strongest</u> as a <u>group</u>, so they <u>behave similarly</u> in an attempt to convince the judges:

© Xinhua / Alamy Stock Photo

Here, the girls are all using the same gesture.

- The actors might <u>huddle together</u> and <u>synchronise</u> their <u>movements</u> to show that the girls are <u>working together</u>.
- They may use <u>wide-eyed expressions</u> and <u>high-pitched voices</u> to persuade the judges they're <u>young</u> and <u>naive</u>.
- Later, the girls pretend to see a yellow bird. They may <u>scream</u> or use <u>panicked movements</u> to make their fear appear more <u>convincing</u>. The actors could also <u>point</u> at the 'bird' or <u>stare</u> at it with <u>disbelieving expressions</u>.

2) Mary eventually <u>buckles</u> under the <u>pressure</u> and accuses Proctor of <u>controlling</u> her through <u>witchcraft</u> — she calls him "the Devil's man" and rushes to join the other girls. In the build-up to this moment, an actor could show that Mary is at <u>breaking point</u> by <u>trembling</u> and <u>looking anxiously</u> around the room.

EXAM TIP

I remember my 'accuse everyone of witchcraft' phase...

Most of the girls don't have many lines, so their physical performance is really important. You need to think carefully about physical skills like facial expressions if you're asked to write about the girls in the exam.

Character Performance — Other Characters

There are plenty of minor characters in *The Crucible*. They might not have as many lines as the big hitters like Proctor, Elizabeth and Abigail, but you could still be asked how you would perform them on stage.

Thomas Putnam is quick to accuse others...

1) Putnam is a rich landowner who thinks that he's intellectually "superior" to the other villagers. He might behave with an air of authority by taking centre stage, or speaking at a louder volume than other characters.

2) He's motivated by greed — he sees the trials as a chance to settle scores and secure land that he believes is rightfully his. His "vindictive nature" leads him to use his daughter (Ruth) to accuse other villagers. An actor playing Putnam could act aggressively towards others by standing close to them on stage or even pointing an accusatory finger in their direction.

3) In Act One, he may also show pleasure when Tituba accuses Sarah Good and Goody Osburn by glancing excitedly at the other villagers and nodding.

4) In Act Three, an actor might smirk when Giles accuses him of "killing his neighbours for their land" — this would suggest that he feels untouchable.

© Drew Farrell/Royal Lyceum Theatre

... and Ann Putnam follows his example

1) Ann is Putnam's wife and Ruth's mother. Like Putnam, she's jealous, unkind and greedy.

2) Miller describes her as a "*death-ridden woman*", because seven of her babies have died in childbirth. An actor might move slowly to suggest the deaths are an emotional burden for her.

3) However, Ann gets excited when Goody Osburn (Ann's midwife) is accused of witchcraft in Act One — she senses an opportunity to blame someone else for her children's deaths. At this point, an actor may use animated gestures and shout "I knew it!" in a gleeful tone.

Character Performance — The Putnams

- The Putnams take advantage of the hysteria for personal gain — their eagerness to accuse others of witchcraft alerts the audience to the dangerous nature of the trials.

- When the accusations start, the two actors might exchange a knowing look and each become more enthusiastic to suggest to the audience that their intentions are dishonest.

Francis Nurse is a respected town elder

1) Francis is Rebecca's elderly husband. He's kind and is known as an "*unofficial judge*" in the community.

2) He's accumulated lots of land and wealth in Salem — his status is respected by some, but resented by others.

3) In Act Two, Francis can't believe that his wife has been arrested. He might arrive at Proctor's house with a shocked facial expression to reflect his surprise.

4) In Act Three, he tries convince the judges that Rebecca is a good woman. An actor may urge Danforth to read the opinions of the other villagers using frantic gestures. This would emphasise his desperation to save Rebecca and encourage the audience to feel sympathy for him.

Character Performance — Francis Nurse

- The Putnams are self-serving, but Francis Nurse puts others first — an actor has to make this contrast clear to the audience.

- An actor might express genuine concern for the people who supported Rebecca. For example, he might weep quietly as Act Three progresses to show that he's worried about putting them in danger.

Character Performance — Other Characters

Judge Hathorne is a ruthless prosecutor

1) Hathorne is a Salem judge who assists Danforth as the "_bitter_, _remorseless_" prosecutor during the trials.

2) In Act Three, the audience <u>hears</u> Hathorne's voice before <u>seeing</u> him on stage, so the actor might use a <u>commanding tone</u> and speak at a <u>high volume</u> for his opening lines. This would highlight his <u>authority</u>.

3) He has <u>less authority</u> than Danforth, but <u>more authority</u> than the other characters. An actor may show that he respects Danforth by <u>turning to him</u> and <u>pausing</u> when Danforth starts speaking. On the other hand, he might <u>interrupt</u> other characters <u>forcefully</u> to suggest that he isn't afraid to <u>assert his authority</u>.

4) Hathorne is <u>quick to judge</u> other characters and <u>aggressive</u> when he <u>interrogates</u> them. An actor might <u>stare coldly</u> at the accused with <u>raised eyebrows</u> to suggest that he <u>doesn't believe</u> what they're saying.

Cheever is the court's clerk...

1) As a <u>clerk</u>, Ezekiel Cheever is responsible for <u>summoning</u> people to <u>court</u> and <u>keeping a record</u> of the <u>trials</u>.

2) He's <u>dutiful</u>, so an actor could use <u>bustling movements</u> and <u>respond quickly</u> to the <u>judges' orders</u> to show that he takes <u>pride</u> in his role.

3) However, Cheever finds it <u>difficult</u> to perform his duties at times — he's "_embarrassed_" when he sees the poppet in Act Two and speaks to Proctor "_apologetically_" in Act Three. An actor could communicate his <u>awkwardness</u> by looking to the floor <u>sheepishly</u> at Proctor's feet.

4) Cheever describes the <u>weight</u> of his role as "_tonnage_" that he carries on his <u>back</u>, so an actor might also put on a <u>slightly stooped posture</u>.

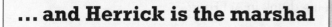

© CATHERINE ASHMORE

... and Herrick is the marshal

1) As the <u>marshal</u> in Salem, Herrick is responsible for <u>arresting</u> the <u>accused</u> and <u>looking after them</u> in <u>jail</u>.

2) He has a <u>busy stage presence</u> and he's often seen <u>escorting prisoners</u> on or offstage. An actor could position themselves <u>upstage</u> and <u>behind</u> the action to show that he's <u>always ready</u> to perform his duties.

> **Character Performance — Cheever and Herrick**
>
> Both men believe that their <u>responsibilities</u> should come <u>first</u>. In performance, actors might use <u>calm</u> and <u>efficient movements</u> to reflect their <u>strict adherence</u> to their <u>duties</u>.

3) He's sometimes <u>reluctant</u> to do his job and feels <u>sorry</u> for those he's arresting — he's "_shamefaced_" when he arrives to arrest Elizabeth. An actor playing Herrick might <u>avoid Elizabeth's gaze</u> as he takes her away.

4) He's "_nearly drunk_" in Act Four, so an actor could <u>move unsteadily</u> and <u>slur his words</u>. His drunkenness might also be interpreted as a sign that he's <u>guilty</u> about his role in the trials and wants to <u>forget</u> about it.

What shall we do with the drunken jailor...?

Imagine you're directing Act Two in a performance of 'The Crucible'. Write instructions for the actors playing Ezekiel Cheever and Marshal Herrick. In your instructions, you should:

1) Refer to specific moments in Act Two.
2) Give detailed examples of performance skills.
3) Explain why your ideas are important and what effect you want them to have on the audience.

Tick list:
✓ knowledge and understanding of the play
✓ physical and vocal skills
✓ effect on the audience

Practice Questions

That was a hefty section, but hopefully by now you've got a pretty good idea of how you could perform each of the characters in 'The Crucible'. Now it's time to put your knowledge to the test with these practice questions.

Quick Questions

1) Give one reason why John Proctor is disliked by some people in Salem.

2) What type of build might an actor playing John Proctor have? Explain why.

3) Who is being described in the line below?
   "It's a bitter woman, a lying, cold, snivelling woman..."

4) Why is Elizabeth conflicted about Proctor's decision to sacrifice himself in Act Four?

5) Give one aspect of Abigail's back story that might explain the way she behaves in the play.

6) Find three quotes from the text to show that Hale is deeply religious.

7) Why is Reverend Parris worried about Betty's 'illness' in Act One?

8) Why doesn't Danforth admit that he was deceived by the girls?

9) Explain why Tituba might be considered as an outsider in Salem.

10) How could an actor portray Marshal Herrick as being drunk in Act Four?

In-depth Questions

1) How might an actor playing Proctor use physical performance to attract sympathy in Act Four?

2) How could an actor playing Elizabeth express her distrust for Proctor in Act Two?

3) Explain how an actor might use performance skills to communicate Abigail's youth and beauty to the audience.

4) How does Reverend Hale's attitude to the witch trials change throughout the play? How might this be reflected in performance?

5) Give three ways in which Danforth's authority might be conveyed to the audience.

6) Using a combination of physical and vocal skills, explain how the actors playing Abigail, Betty, Mercy Lewis and Mary Warren might interact with each other in Act One.

Practice Questions

Now it's time to put on your performance hat and get those creative juices flowing with some more exam-style questions. The key to exam success is practice, practice, practice — so don't be tempted to skip any questions on this page that look tricky. For each question you answer, you should aim to write at least three paragraphs.

Exam-style Questions

> Find the part of Act One where Proctor and Abigail are alone together. Read from where Abigail says "**Gah! I'd almost forgot how strong you are, John Proctor!**" to where Proctor says "**Do you look for whippin'?**", then answer Questions 1 and 2 below.

1) Imagine you're a performer playing Proctor. Discuss how you would use your performance skills to portray him in this extract. You should explain why your ideas are suitable for this extract and for the rest of the play.

2) Reread the last part of the extract, from "**Abby, I may think of you softly from time to time**" to the final line.

   Imagine you're a performer playing Abigail. Explain how you and the performer playing John Proctor might use the space on stage and interact together to create tension for the audience in this part of the extract.

> Find the part of Act Three where Proctor presents Mary's deposition to Danforth. Read from "***Proctor starts to hand Danforth the deposition***" to where Hale says "**I surely do not, sir. Let you consider it, then**", then answer Questions 3 and 4 below.

3) Imagine you're directing a production of *The Crucible*. Explain how a performer playing the character of Hale might demonstrate his troubled conscience to the audience in this extract and elsewhere in the play.

4) Imagine you're a performer playing Danforth. Describe how you would perform the line "**Mr Hale, you surely do not doubt my justice**" using your vocal and physical skills. You should explain the effects you want to create.

> Find the part of Act Four where Reverend Parris reveals that Abigail has run away. Read from where Danforth says "**Mr Parris, be plain, what troubles you?**" to where Reverend Parris says "**There is danger for me. I dare not step outside at night!**", then answer Question 5.

5) Imagine you're a performer playing Reverend Parris. Discuss how you would use your performance skills to portray him in this extract. You should explain why your ideas are suitable for this extract and for the rest of the play.

Section Four — Staging and Design

Stage Types and Stage Design

It's important to pick an appropriate stage type and design a performance space that works for the whole play.

'The Crucible' can be staged in different ways

1) Directors of *The Crucible* should think about the style of their production when choosing a stage type.

2) *The Crucible* was written to be staged and performed in a naturalistic style (see p.20). In naturalistic productions the stage is often set back from the audience, which helps to maintain the 'fourth wall' (the imagined barrier between the audience and the actors). This can add to the illusion that the audience are observing real life playing out on stage.

3) A non-naturalistic production of *The Crucible* might use a stage type that brings the actors closer to the audience, making it easier for them to break the fourth wall.

4) The director needs to make sure the performance space is suitable for staging all four acts of the play — Miller gives detailed stage directions that describe the layout and features of different settings, so directors should consider these requirements when deciding which stage type to use.

> **Non-naturalistic Theatre**
>
> Non-naturalistic theatre includes features that suggest to the audience that what they're watching isn't real. In a production of *The Crucible*, this might encourage the audience to think carefully about the play's messages, rather than focusing so much on its plot.

Different stage types can create different effects

1) **Proscenium arch** and **end-on staging** let the director use backdrops and large pieces of scenery. Miller's stage directions describe settings that look like real places, so a director might want to use scenery and backdrops to make the settings seem really vivid and realistic.

> These stage types can make it harder for the audience to see the actors' facial expressions, which might reduce the emotional impact of the play.

2) **Thrust staging** can be used to create an intimate atmosphere. Staging key emotional scenes (like Elizabeth and Proctor's final conversation in Act Four) on the apron would give the audience a clearer view of the actors, which would make it easier for them to feel the emotion of the scene.

3) **Traverse staging** positions the audience so they are looking at one another across the stage. This could intensify the claustrophobic mood of *The Crucible* by reminding the audience that people in Salem were always watching each other's actions.

4) **Theatre in the round** can create a very intense atmosphere, as the audience completely surrounds the actors. Using this staging might help the audience experience the hysteria of the witch trials.

5) **Promenade theatre** helps the audience feel more involved in the play because they move with the actors to different settings. This could add to the mood of uncertainty and tension in *The Crucible* because the audience would be unsure about where they might be taken next.

> **Practical Issues**
>
> Directors need to consider the practicalities of the stage type they choose. For example, set changes can be tricky when staging the play in the round. Directors also need to think about how the audience's line of sight (their view of the action on stage) will be affected by the type of staging they use. Otherwise, there's a danger that the impact of key moments in the play, such as John Proctor's "Because it is my name!" speech, could be lost.

This production was staged in the round. It used a very simple set to ensure that audience members on all sides of the stage had a clear line of sight.

Stage Types and Stage Design

Staging and performance space are linked

1) Using a small performance space would make the actors seem crowded together in busy scenes like the end of Act One. This could be used to create a claustrophobic or frantic atmosphere.

2) A large space could be useful for creating clear lines of sight between the audience and each actor on stage. This would help to make the actions and reactions of each character clearly visible during Act Three when lots of characters are on stage at once.

3) A director should also consider how different areas of the stage might be used for effect. To help with this, directors often imagine the stage as being split up into nine areas. When the audience is on more than one side, directors still picture the stage like this — they pick one side of the audience as their focus.

4) The location of characters on the stage helps to shape the relationship between the audience and the actors. The audience is likely to pay more attention to characters who are standing downstage, so they will seem more important.

5) In Act Three, the stage layout could be used to focus the audience's attention on the accused villagers. A judges' bench could be upstage left and stools for the villagers could be downstage right. This would encourage the audience to sympathise with the victims.

Upstage Right (USR)	Upstage Centre (USC)	Upstage Left (USL)
Stage Right (SR)	Centre Stage (CS)	Stage Left (SL)
Downstage Right (DSR)	Downstage Centre (DSC)	Downstage Left (DSL)

AUDIENCE

This production uses the position of stage furniture to clearly separate the accused from the judges.

Entrances and exits can have dramatic impact

1) Miller describes the location of entrances and exits for each setting in his stage directions (see p.22-23). A director should consider how to build them into their stage design.

2) Directors don't have to follow Miller's stage directions, but they should still consider how to create the dramatic effects that Miller intended when designing their own entrances and exits.

3) For example, in Act Four, Danforth's footsteps can be heard offstage as he approaches the prison cell. The actor playing Danforth could approach the stage along a darkened walkway through the audience — this would build a similar sense of anticipation.

4) Entrances and exits can also be designed to create symbolism. In a non-naturalistic production, John Proctor could exit the stage through a trapdoor at the end of Act Four. Trapdoors are associated with gallows, so this would symbolise that he is going to his death.

The Doorway in Act Two

In Act Two, the doorway leading "outside" could be positioned at an angle to the wings at the end of a flat — it would be clearly visible to the audience, but would conceal actors approaching it from the wings. This would add to the dramatic impact when Hale suddenly appears in the doorway.

My fashion sense means I'm often left feeling upstaged...

Imagine that you are staging the play in the round. Draw a sketch that shows how you'd design the entrances and exits for Act Three. Make sure you include annotations that explain:

1) How the entrances and exits would be positioned.
2) What the audience would and would not be able to see.
3) The dramatic effects your design would create.

If you have time, you could also draw similar sketches for the other acts in the play. Don't forget to think about the dramatic impact of your designs.

Set Design

Set designers use scenery to create effective settings that get across the messages and themes of *The Crucible*.

Set design should support the style of the production

1) Each act in *The Crucible* is set in a different room — Betty Parris's <u>bedroom</u>, the Proctors' <u>living room</u>, a room at the <u>court</u> and a <u>prison cell</u>. The <u>design</u> of these settings should match the <u>overall style</u> of the production (see p.20).

2) A <u>naturalistic</u> production would use a <u>historically accurate</u> set design to recreate 17th-century Salem <u>realistically</u> (see p.7), adding to the <u>illusion</u> that the audience are watching <u>real life</u>.

3) <u>Non-naturalistic</u> productions aren't realistic. They encourage the audience to focus on the <u>messages</u> of the play instead of immersing them in the <u>story</u> and its <u>historical setting</u>.

4) One way of achieving this would be to use a <u>minimalist set design</u> with elements of <u>symbolism</u> to highlight the <u>themes</u> of the play. For example, the <u>court setting</u> could be communicated <u>symbolically</u> — a silhouette of a <u>pair of scales</u> (which are a symbol of <u>justice</u>) could be printed on a <u>backdrop</u>.

The details of a set design can reinforce a setting...

1) A <u>naturalistic design</u> might create the impression that <u>authentic materials</u> have been used. The designer would have to make their set look <u>realistic</u>, while still ensuring that it could be <u>moved easily</u>.

| MATERIALS | • Many buildings in 17th-century Salem were made of <u>wood</u>. A naturalistic set design for the <u>houses</u> and the <u>court</u> might have walls that appear to be <u>timber-clad</u>.
• The wood could be made to look like it has a <u>coarse texture</u> to make these settings feel more <u>rustic</u>.
• The walls of the prison cell might look like <u>rough stone</u> and the floor could be scattered with <u>straw</u> to emphasise the <u>oppressive</u>, <u>uncomfortable</u> nature of the prison. |

| COLOUR | By using materials like wood and stone, the designer would make the <u>colours</u> of their set <u>muted and dull</u>. This would reflect the serious <u>Puritan lifestyle</u> of 17th-century Salem. |

2) Designers also need to think about the <u>shape</u> of the set. In Act One, the "*roof rafters*" are exposed, suggesting the room's in the <u>attic</u> — the <u>upper walls</u> could come together in a <u>triangular shape</u> to show this.

... and they can also create symbolism

1) Symbolism can be incorporated into the <u>scenery</u>. In Act One, a <u>large cross</u> could be put on the back wall of the bedroom to symbolise Reverend Parris's obsession with his <u>reputation</u> as a <u>religious</u> man.

2) <u>Colour symbolism</u> (see p.52) can also highlight key themes, especially in non-naturalistic productions.

| SCALE | • <u>Non-naturalistic</u> set designs may use <u>unrealistic scale</u> to <u>emphasise</u> aspects of the play to the audience. Using <u>oversized scenery</u> could make the actors on stage appear <u>smaller</u>, which would emphasise their <u>inability</u> to <u>fight the forces</u> in the play that are <u>beyond their control</u>.
• In Act One, a designer could change the <u>scale</u> of Betty's bedroom so its <u>dimensions</u> are all <u>mismatched</u>, creating an <u>unsettling effect</u> that symbolises the <u>uncertainty</u> that the girls' accusations will cause. |

This production uses a dark red backdrop to symbolise the danger of the trials.

Set Design

Levels can be practical and symbolic

Miller's <u>stage directions</u> don't describe stage <u>levels</u>, but a director can still include them in their <u>set design</u>.

1) <u>Rostra</u> (raised platforms) can <u>highlight</u> key moments in the play. In Act Four, Proctor could stand on a <u>rostrum</u> at <u>centre stage</u> when he rips up his <u>confession</u>. This would <u>emphasise</u> the importance of the moment and ensure that <u>everyone</u> in the audience would be able to <u>see</u> what he has done.

2) Levels can also be used to <u>separate</u> different <u>areas</u> of a <u>setting</u>. In Act One, Betty's bedroom could be <u>elevated</u> above the stage. This <u>higher level</u> could be accessed by the "<u>stairway</u>" leading from the bedroom to the <u>ground floor</u> of Parris's house.

3) Levels can also show <u>relationships</u> between characters. For example, <u>authority figures</u> like Danforth and Hathorne could be positioned at a <u>higher level</u> than the accused characters in Act Three to <u>symbolise</u> their <u>higher status</u>, and to show the <u>power</u> they hold over the other characters.

This production positioned the set for Betty's bedroom on the roof of Parris's house to elevate it above the stage.

Technical devices can make it easier to stage 'The Crucible'...

Technical devices might be built into the set design for <u>practical</u> reasons:

1) <u>Trucks</u> (see p.81) could be used to <u>quickly change</u> the <u>set</u> between Act Two and Act Three. The Proctors' "*low*" <u>living room</u> is replaced by the <u>meeting house vestry</u>, which has "*two high windows*". The <u>walls</u> of these settings could be shown using <u>trucks</u> so they can be <u>easily moved</u> on and off the stage.

2) Parts of the background could be <u>painted</u> onto <u>flats</u> to create the impression that authentic materials like wood and stone have been used. This saves the production from having to actually use these materials, which might be <u>expensive</u> or <u>difficult to move</u>.

... and they can be used for dramatic effect

> Set designers need to make sure that any special effects fit in with the overall style of the production.

Technical devices can also create <u>special effects</u> on stage.

Technical Device	Potential use in *The Crucible*	Dramatic Effect
Projectors	Silhouettes of <u>a dark forest</u> and <u>swinging nooses</u> could be projected onto a backdrop when the girls make <u>accusations</u> in Act One.	This would create a <u>dark</u> and <u>unsettling</u> <u>mood</u> to reflect the <u>dangerous</u> nature of the girls' accusations. It would also <u>foreshadow</u> the <u>deaths</u> that they cause later in the play.
Smoke machines	Smoke machines could be used to release <u>light mist</u> onto the stage before <u>Hale's arrival</u> in Act Two.	The <u>growing mist</u> on stage would increase the <u>tension</u> and <u>mask</u> Hale's approach so he enters the stage "*as though from the air*".
Flying rigs	When Betty tries to <u>fly</u> and "*streaks*" towards the window in Act One, the actor playing her could be <u>lifted</u> in the air slightly using a <u>flying rig</u>.	This would make the action more <u>visually dramatic</u> by making Betty's movements seem <u>fluid</u> and <u>weightless</u>, as though she's about to <u>take off</u>.
Pyrotechnics	Pyrotechnics could be used to create the <u>Proctors' fire</u> in Act Two. The fire could <u>flare up</u> briefly when Mary says "The Devil's loose in Salem".	Having a <u>real fire</u> would make the setting feel more <u>realistic</u>. Making the fire flare up at the mention of the <u>Devil</u> would create a <u>symbolic</u> link between <u>Salem</u> and <u>hell</u>.

Set Design

Different elements of set design work together

1) The overall set design needs to support the production <u>style</u>. If the style is <u>naturalistic</u>, the set design should include naturalistic features <u>throughout</u> the play.

2) The atmosphere of *The Crucible* is <u>oppressive</u> — the play's settings could all be designed to show this. For example, the designer could make each setting appear <u>low</u> or <u>narrow</u> to create an impression of <u>confinement</u>.

3) The way that the set <u>changes</u> over the course of the play could communicate important <u>ideas</u>. The walls of each new setting in the play could be brought in so that there is <u>less space</u> on the stage in each act. This would emphasise the <u>oppressive atmosphere</u> of the play and create the impression that Proctor's fate is <u>slowly closing in</u> on him.

4) Changes in the set could also show how the <u>mood</u> of the play changes. The mood in Act Three is more <u>serious</u> and <u>threatening</u> than in the first two acts. A director could show this by making the meeting house seem <u>colder</u> and more <u>unwelcoming</u> than Betty's bedroom and the Proctors' living room. For example, they could use a very <u>empty set</u> without any colour and create <u>jagged angles</u> to represent the *"heavy beams"* that *"jut out"*.

This set for the Proctors' house creates a sense of confinement by using walls to box the characters in.

© Donald Cooper/photostage

Explain the ideas behind your set design

When you're writing about set design in the exam, it's important to <u>explain why</u> you'd design the set in a <u>certain way</u>. Here's an example of how you could write about the <u>design of a setting</u>:

> This considers the effect on the <u>audience</u>.

> This gives <u>precise details</u> about <u>technical devices</u>.

In Act One, Betty's bedroom gives off an *"air of clean sparseness"*. To create this effect and to highlight the simplicity of the Puritan lifestyle for the audience, I would keep the walls of the bedroom plain, without any decoration. I would also construct the walls from flats painted to look like they were timber-clad. This would reflect the Puritan style of simple wooden buildings that was common in 17th-century Salem, which would make the setting seem authentic for the audience.

> This explains the <u>overall effect</u> that you hope to achieve.

The Devil isn't in Salem — he's in the detail...

REVISION TASK

Imagine you're staging a naturalistic production of 'The Crucible'. Write a short paragraph that describes the scenery you'd use to create the meeting house setting in Act Three. Think about:

1) The materials, textures and colours you'd use.
2) The overall atmosphere you're trying to create.
3) Why your choices are suitable for a naturalistic production of *The Crucible*.

Tick list:
✓ specific design details
✓ how historical context can influence design choices
✓ the effect on the audience

Props and Stage Furniture

No matter how pretty they look, props and stage furniture aren't just for decoration — they help the audience understand key details about the play's settings, themes and characters. Now that's what I call multi-tasking...

Props and stage furniture help to communicate setting...

1) In a naturalistic production, a set designer would use props and stage furniture to show that the play is set in 17th-century Salem. They would choose materials and colours that were commonly used at that time and include furniture that is plain and functional to communicate the Puritans' simple lifestyle.

2) Designers can use props to reveal extra information about the play's settings. At the start of Act Two, objects like the cooking pot, ladle, plate and glass establish the domestic nature of the setting for the audience.

3) In Act Three, the Salem meeting house (a place of worship) is used as the village court house. A set designer might use pews for the "plain" benches that are on either side of the vestry room to emphasise the religious function of the meeting house.

In this scene, props like the quill and the copyholder help to emphasise the formality of the court proceedings.

... and they can also create symbolism

1) Some props are symbols. In Act Four, Elizabeth enters wearing a "heavy chain" around her wrists — this prop symbolises her lack of freedom. The way the chain would limit the actor's movements before it is removed would also act as a visual reminder of Elizabeth's lack of power at this point in the play.

2) Symbolic effect can also be created by the way props and stage furniture are designed:

- The size of a prop can create symbolism. In Act Two, the needle in the "poppet" could be large and prominent, to symbolise the clear threat of violence posed by the witch trials.

- Colour can also be symbolic. In a non-naturalistic production, all of the stage furniture in the meeting house in Act Three could be white to symbolise the artificial and clinical nature of the trials.

Important props might also be made slightly larger so they're more recognisable to the audience.

Personal props can reinforce characterisation

A personal prop is a prop that is used by an actor to add depth to their character:

1) Proctor's "whip" highlights the control that he has over his family. The position of this prop, which is initially hanging on the mantel, signifies that Proctor values his role as head of the household.

2) Props can also be used to indicate a character's status. In Act One, Hale enters carrying "half a dozen heavy books" that he claims are "weighted with authority". These props immediately characterise Hale as a man who is proud of his education and wants to make it known to those around him.

Make sure you have a prop-er good read of this page...

If you're writing about prop and stage furniture design for *The Crucible*, you need to be able to explain how small details like the materials of these features, or their colour and size, might affect the audience.

Lighting

Lighting designers use lighting effects to support the story that the director wants to tell. Illuminating stuff...

Miller describes the lighting for each setting

1) Miller includes references to <u>naturalistic lighting</u> in his <u>stage directions</u> about each setting (see p.22). There is "<u>*morning sunlight*</u>" in Betty's room in Act One, and "<u>*moonlight*</u>" seeps into the jail in Act Four.

2) This lighting has a <u>practical role</u> — it tells the audience the <u>time of day</u> when each act is <u>set</u>.

3) Although Miller says what <u>type of light</u> should appear on stage in each act, he doesn't describe <u>every</u> aspect of lighting design, and he doesn't explain <u>how</u> the lighting effects should be created. This gives the <u>director</u> and <u>designer</u> some freedom to make their own decisions.

4) A <u>non-naturalistic</u> production might not follow Miller's stage directions about lighting at all, which would give the designer even more <u>creative freedom</u>.

Lighting design should match the style of the production

1) The lighting for a <u>naturalistic production</u> of *The Crucible* should make the settings seem <u>realistic</u>.

2) Designers might create the impression of <u>real light sources</u> on stage that would have been common in 17th-century Salem, such as <u>candles</u>, <u>fires</u> and <u>lanterns</u>. Their lighting effects could <u>mimic</u> the light given off by these sources.

3) For example, in Act Two, the Proctors' living room is "*dark*", but a <u>fire</u> is burning in the fireplace. A <u>Fresnel</u> (see p.80) shone through an <u>orange-tinted gel</u> could be used to cast a <u>soft orange light</u> in the <u>fireplace</u> to suggest firelight.

4) Lighting designers have more <u>freedom</u> when lighting a <u>non-naturalistic</u> production because onstage lighting doesn't have to create a <u>realistic</u> impression. A designer might use <u>surreal lighting</u> effects to heighten moments of <u>tension</u>. For example, at the end of Act One, <u>strobe lighting</u> could be used to hint that Salem has begun to descend into <u>chaos</u>.

© Donald Cooper/photostage

Colour can establish features of a setting

1) The colour of lighting can create an impression of the <u>temperature</u> of a setting. <u>Blue light</u> can be used to suggest <u>coldness</u> — in Act Four, the jail could be lit with a <u>blue wash</u> to make it seem <u>chilly</u>.

2) Colour can also be used to indicate <u>time of day</u>. For example, <u>dark purple light</u> can be used to suggest <u>darkness</u> — in Act Two, the <u>doorway</u> of the Proctors' house could be lit with purple light to show that it is <u>almost dark outside</u>.

3) Pale white light can suggest moonlight — at the start of Act Four, a <u>gobo</u> (see p.80) attached to a white <u>profile spotlight</u> could be used to project a silhouette of <u>prison bars</u> onto the prison wall to give the impression that "<u>*moonlight*</u>" is coming into the cell.

4) Warm colours can suggest sunlight — as the "<u>*new sun*</u>" rises at the end of the play, <u>floodlights</u> with pink and orange <u>gels</u> attached could be used to gradually fill the stage with <u>warm light</u> to show that <u>dawn</u> has arrived.

5) <u>Non-naturalistic</u> productions of *The Crucible* are more likely to use colour <u>symbolically</u>. For example, <u>red light</u> can be used to symbolise <u>danger</u>. In Act Four, the stage could be flooded with red light at the moment when Proctor is <u>hanged</u>.

Colour symbolism

Colour symbolism uses the <u>feelings</u> and <u>ideas</u> that are associated with certain <u>colours</u> to create <u>meaning</u> for the audience.

Lighting

Lighting can support characterisation

1) Lighting can be used to <u>emphasise</u> the <u>qualities</u> of a particular <u>character</u>. When Abigail is interrogated by Parris in Act One, <u>backlighting</u> could be used to place her in <u>shadow</u>. This could suggest that there's something <u>sinister</u> about her, making her seem <u>less trustworthy</u> to the audience.

2) Lighting is also useful for revealing a character's <u>status</u>. When Danforth is questioning Mary in Act Three, <u>downlighting</u> at a <u>shallow angle</u> could be used to cast a <u>large shadow</u> behind the actor playing him. This would <u>increase</u> Danforth's <u>presence</u> on stage, emphasising his <u>power</u> over the other characters at this point in the play.

3) The <u>relationship</u> between characters can also be <u>reinforced</u> through lighting. For example, when Proctor stands at the doorway and Elizabeth is at the table in Act Two, <u>barndoors</u> (see p.80) could be used to cast a <u>shadow</u> between the table and the doorway. This would emphasise the <u>emotional distance</u> between them. The <u>width</u> of this shadow could be <u>slowly expanded</u> when a "*sense of their separation rises*".

4) A character's <u>emotions</u> can be <u>revealed</u> using lighting. When Parris first enters in Act Four, he is "*frightened*". A <u>side light</u> could be shone on his <u>upper body</u> to make his <u>facial features</u> more <u>visible</u>. This would emphasise his fearful expression, making his <u>agitation</u> clearer to the audience.

5) A <u>non-naturalistic production</u> might use lighting <u>symbolically</u> to support <u>characterisation</u>:

   - In Act Two, a <u>Fresnel</u> could be used to cast a <u>soft</u>, <u>white</u> light on Elizabeth when she is accused of witchcraft to emphasise her <u>innocence</u> and <u>goodness</u> to the audience.
   - When Elizabeth is "*pouring out her heart*" to Proctor in Act Four, the <u>brightness</u> of the lighting could be slowly <u>intensified</u> to highlight her <u>rising emotions</u>.

Lighting contributes to the play's atmosphere

1) The <u>colour</u> of lighting can affect the atmosphere on stage. When Mary recalls feeling a "misty coldness" creeping up her spine in Act Two, a <u>wash</u> of <u>pale blue light</u> could create an <u>eerie atmosphere</u>.

2) Lighting can contribute to the atmosphere of a <u>setting</u>. In Act Two, <u>birdies</u> (see p.80) concealed within the <u>set</u> could be used to cast a <u>soft pool of light</u> around the fireplace to show the warmth of the fire.

3) The <u>brightness</u> of lighting can be used to create a <u>tense atmosphere</u> on stage. In Act Three, when Danforth tries to <u>force</u> Mary to confess, the stage could be lit with a <u>pale white wash</u>. This lighting could gradually increase in <u>intensity</u> as Danforth becomes more <u>aggressive</u> towards Mary, contributing to the <u>tense atmosphere</u> that rises during this scene.

4) In Act Four, the stage could be lit with a <u>dim wash</u> and the <u>edges</u> of the cell could be in <u>shadow</u> to emphasise the "*darkness*" in the prison. This would help to create an <u>ominous atmosphere</u>.

5) <u>Changes</u> in lighting can indicate a <u>shift</u> in <u>mood</u>. In Act Four when Proctor <u>confesses</u>, the stage could be lit with a <u>mixture</u> of <u>warm</u> and <u>cool</u> tones. When Proctor leaves to be hanged, the <u>warmer tones</u> could be <u>dimmed</u> to create <u>cooler lighting</u> that reflects the increasingly <u>tragic atmosphere</u> of the act.

This outdoor production of 'The Crucible' used a spotlight to illuminate trees behind the stage, creating an eerie atmosphere.

Special Effects

Special <u>lighting effects</u> can add to atmosphere. When the girls pretend to be <u>bewitched</u> in Act Three, <u>strobe lights</u> could be used to make their <u>movements</u> seem <u>jerky</u> and <u>unnatural</u>. This would create a <u>surreal atmosphere</u> that reflects Danforth's belief that the girls are under the <u>influence</u> of the <u>supernatural</u>.

Lighting

Lighting helps to highlight the action on stage...

1) As well as creating meaning for the audience, lighting is <u>essential</u> for making sure that the audience can <u>see</u> what is <u>happening</u>.

2) It can also be used to <u>direct</u> the audience's <u>attention</u> to a specific part of the stage:

Lighting directors mustn't just focus on specific parts of the stage. Considering the lighting of the stage as a whole is important too.

- In Act One, Betty could be lit with a sharp-edged, <u>profile spotlight</u> as she lies *"inert"* on the bed. This would draw attention to her <u>unusual stillness</u>.
- In Act Two, lights could be attached to the wall around the mantel so the <u>poppet</u> is <u>clearly visible</u> to the audience when Cheever says "I spy a poppet".
- A spotlight could <u>follow</u> the <u>warrant</u> in Act Two when Proctor <u>snatches</u> it from Cheever and <u>tears</u> it up so that it's <u>obvious</u> what has happened.

... and it enhances the impact of key moments

© KS-Fotografie/action press/REX/Shutterstock

1) During the <u>interrogation</u> of Tituba in Act One, <u>uplighting</u> could be used to cast <u>strange shadows</u> on Hale, Parris and Ann Putnam's faces to make them seem <u>more intimidating</u>.

2) When Hale <u>condemns</u> the court and <u>exits</u> the stage in Act Three, a <u>blackout</u> could occur as he *"slams the door"*. This would make Hale's exit seem <u>more shocking</u> because the darkness would intensify the <u>fear</u> and <u>uncertainty</u> for the audience.

3) When Elizabeth enters the jail cell in Act Four, the <u>doorway</u> could be lit from <u>above</u> so that the actor's <u>costume</u> is clearly visible. This would highlight her *"dirty"* <u>clothes</u> and her *"pale and gaunt"* <u>face</u>, showing how much she has <u>suffered</u> while she's been in <u>prison</u>.

Use technical terms to write about lighting

When you're writing about using lighting to <u>emphasise</u> a character's <u>emotions</u>, it's important to explain the details of your lighting design. Here is an example:

Give <u>precise details</u> about the lighting equipment you'd use.

This gives the <u>intended effect</u> on the audience.

When Tituba makes her false confession at the end of Act One, I'd train a profile spotlight on the actor and dim the lighting rigged above the performance space to cast the rest of the stage into shadow. This would clearly highlight to the audience the fact that Tituba is *"weeping"*. The candle near Betty's bed would be an electric candle, which I'd programme to flicker on and off during Tituba's false confession. This would hint at her erratic and disturbed emotional state.

This explains the <u>reason</u> for the lighting choice.

Many (stage)hands make light work...

When you're writing about lighting design in the exam, make sure that all of your ideas will work together as a whole. Each idea should contribute to the overall style and impression that you're trying to create.

Section Four — Staging and Design

Sound

Sound designers are in charge of all the sound in a play — apart from the audience's ~~booing~~ applause that is...

Sound designers should consider the director's vision

1) Miller <u>doesn't</u> include much information about sound in the <u>stage directions</u> for *The Crucible*.

2) Although this gives sound designers the opportunity to be <u>creative</u>, it's important that the sound design is still <u>in keeping</u> with the director's <u>vision</u> and complements the <u>style</u> of the production.

3) When designers create a <u>sound plot</u>, they'll want to think about how sound can:

• convey the <u>setting</u> and <u>context</u>	• create <u>tension</u> and <u>mood</u>
• convey <u>actions on and offstage</u>	• create <u>symbolism</u>
• emphasise <u>characterisation</u>	• emphasise <u>Miller's message</u>

> A sound plot is a plan that contains a list of all the sounds and sound equipment used for a production. It also says when the sounds will be used.

The play's setting and context can be reflected in its sound

1) *The Crucible* is set in <u>rural</u> Massachusetts. In a <u>naturalistic</u> production, a sound designer could help to establish this <u>setting</u> for the audience by playing a <u>pre-recorded</u> <u>soundscape</u> of bird-song, cows lowing and distant villagers chatting when the curtain rises at the start of Act One.

> A soundscape is a collection of individual sounds that are layered up to give a strong sense of place. They help to establish setting, as the audience associates what they hear with a certain type of place.

2) A sound designer could also emphasise the <u>religious</u> context of the play. In Act One, while Proctor and Abigail discuss their <u>affair</u>, a "*psalm*" is being sung downstairs. Having this <u>hymn</u> clearly playing in the background would emphasise the importance of <u>Christianity</u> in <u>Puritan society</u> and draw attention to the <u>sinful</u> nature of their <u>affair</u>.

3) At the start of Act Three, the "*roaring*" of "*townspeople*" excited by the trial takes place <u>offstage</u>. Using <u>surround sound</u> (playing sound through multiple speakers that surround the audience) would help to reflect the <u>claustrophobic</u> society of <u>17th-century Salem</u>, where people's <u>private lives</u> were <u>closely followed</u> by the rest of the community.

Sound can reinforce actions

1) Sound can be used to <u>emphasise</u> what is happening <u>on stage</u> in the play, for example a knock on a door. These sounds are normally <u>diegetic</u> (sounds that the characters can <u>hear</u>) and can be <u>live</u> or <u>pre-recorded</u>.

2) <u>Offstage sound effects</u> can be used to suggest that action is happening <u>elsewhere</u>. For example, when Elizabeth exits the stage in Act Two after her arrest, the audience hears "*Horses and a wagon creaking*". This tells the audience that Elizabeth is being <u>transported to the jail</u>. It's much easier to <u>suggest</u> this to the audience using sound effects than to <u>show</u> it on stage.

> **Effect on the Audience**
>
> Offstage sound effects are also normally <u>diegetic</u>. They are often used in <u>naturalistic</u> productions to make the play seem more <u>believable</u> — they encourage the audience to accept that the events on stage are taking place within a <u>wider world</u> beyond the stage.

3) As well as <u>conveying actions</u> to the audience, sound can also be used to highlight the <u>importance</u> of an action. For example, in Act Two, Proctor <u>rips up</u> the warrant for Elizabeth's arrest. A sound designer may choose to <u>amplify</u> the tearing sound to make Proctor's action seem more <u>dramatic</u>.

Sound

Characterisation can be emphasised by sound

1) In productions of *The Crucible*, <u>characterisation</u> is usually created by the actors' <u>performances</u>, as well as their <u>costumes</u>. However, some directors may also use <u>sound</u> to add to characterisation.

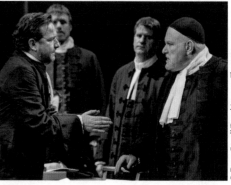

2) For example, the <u>entrance</u> of Danforth and Hathorne in Act Four may be <u>announced</u> with a <u>chime</u> of a <u>heavy bell</u>. The ringing of a bell is often seen as an <u>omen</u> of <u>death</u>, so the sound would emphasise their roles in the <u>executions</u>.

3) <u>Silence</u> can be just as <u>powerful</u> as sound. In Act One, "*Everything is quiet*" as Rebecca Nurse goes to <u>soothe</u> Betty. The use of silence during this noisy scene makes the moment stand out and emphasises Rebecca's <u>gentle</u> and <u>peaceful</u> nature.

© Drew Farrell/Royal Lyceum Theatre

Sound can add to mood and tension

1) Miller doesn't give any instructions about <u>non-diegetic sounds</u> in his stage directions. A sound designer might use some as they are an effective way of creating a certain <u>mood</u> or adding to the <u>tension</u> of a scene:

> **Non-diegetic Sounds**
>
> Non-diegetic sounds are sounds that exist <u>outside</u> the world of the <u>play</u> and <u>aren't heard</u> by <u>characters</u>. They include <u>voice-overs</u> and <u>incidental music</u>.

- While Parris kneels by Betty's bed in Act One, <u>underscoring</u> (playing <u>incidental music</u> quietly during a scene) with <u>melancholy</u> music could suggest that something <u>isn't right</u> and create an <u>uncertain</u> mood.
- In Act Two, the <u>low-pitched</u> sound of a cello being played in a <u>minor key</u> could be used to create an <u>intense</u> atmosphere when Proctor <u>struggles with</u> Mary and tries to make her confess she has been lying. The sound could <u>cut off</u> when Mary is thrown to the floor to heighten the <u>tension</u> of the moment.
- When Proctor and Elizabeth are reunited in Act Four, <u>soft</u>, <u>melodic</u> music could reflect the <u>tenderness</u> of the moment. This music could become more <u>sombre</u> as Elizabeth reveals that Giles is dead.

2) As well as using music, a sound designer could use equipment to enhance the <u>actors' voices</u> so they add to the mood. For example, when the girls <u>chant</u> together in Act Three, their voices could be captured by a <u>microphone</u> suspended <u>above</u> the stage. This would <u>amplify</u> their chanting, creating an intense <u>wall of sound</u> that would be <u>disturbing</u> and <u>confusing</u> for the audience.

3) Sound designers can also use <u>equipment</u> to make sound within the play more <u>dramatic</u>. For example, at the end of Act One, a sound designer may use <u>surround sound</u> to project the girls' "*ecstatic cries*" all around the audience. This would make the sound seem more <u>unnatural</u>, making the audience feel <u>uncomfortable</u> and creating a <u>frantic</u> mood.

A designer might use sound symbolically

1) Sound can be used <u>symbolically</u> to convey <u>meaning</u> to the audience.

2) When Elizabeth is arrested in Act Two, the "*clank of chain is heard*". In this scene, the sound of chains symbolises the <u>threat</u> that the witch trials pose to people's <u>freedom</u>, so a sound technician might make the "*clank*" <u>loud</u> and <u>threatening</u> to remind the audience of the <u>sinister</u> nature of the witch trials.

3) The play ends with Proctor being escorted from the jail to be <u>hanged</u>. The audience hears a <u>drum roll</u> offstage which eventually "*heightens violently*" — <u>cutting off</u> this sound <u>suddenly</u> would symbolise the moment of Proctor's tragic <u>death</u>.

Sound

Sound can be linked to the play's message

1) Miller wrote *The Crucible* to highlight the injustice faced by people accused of communism in 1950s America (see p.10-11). A non-naturalistic production could emphasise this message to an audience through sound.

2) For example, a sound designer may include a crackly speech from a 1950s politician which warns about the threat of communism. This audio recording could fade in and out at key moments, such as when the girls begin accusing people.

3) Between Act Two and Act Three, music from 1950s America could be played to accompany a projection showing 1950s headlines relating to McCarthy and communism. This would also make it clearer to the audience that the witch trials about to be shown on stage are a metaphor for McCarthyism.

Part of a speech by Senator McCarthy could be used as an underscore to help create a link to the witch hunts in 1950s America.

Effect on the Audience

Using sounds associated with 1950s America could be an effective way of reminding the audience about the play's message, but it might be jarring if the rest of the play is performed in a naturalistic style.

Be specific about sound in exam answers

When writing about sound in your exam, it's important to give details about how the sounds are made:

> At the end of Act Four, Miller says that the final drum roll "crashes" and that the drums "rattle like bones in the morning air". I would use a live drum roll with a snare drum, as this would create short, sharp sounds that would simulate the rattling effect. This would crescendo to become extremely loud, gradually increasing the tension in the build-up to Proctor's and Rebecca's deaths. The drum would then echo as the lights dim — this echo of the drums might signify to the audience that there are many more to be hanged in Salem.

Use the correct technical terms in your answer.

This shows the effect of sound on the audience.

This gives precise details of how the sound is created.

Sounds like you're ready for some questions...

REVISION TASK

Create a sound plot by choosing an act from 'The Crucible' and making a list of all the sounds you might use for that act. You should think about the following:

1) The sounds you would use, and whether they are live or pre-recorded.

2) The style of your production and how this might affect your choices.

3) The effect the sounds might have on the audience.

Tick list:
✓ different sources of sound
✓ style of production
✓ effect on the audience

Costume

Human piñata, inflatable dinosaur, back end of a pantomime camel — I've had a few excellent costumes over the years. It's difficult to understand why Miller didn't include anything like them in *The Crucible*...

Realistic costumes rely heavily on context

In a naturalistic production of *The Crucible*, the costumes should reflect the play's context to make them seem authentic. Costume designers need to consider the following:

Material

1) Most clothes would have been made out of simple materials that were cheap and readily available — these include wool, linen and felt. These fabrics are thick and durable enough to endure the strenuous jobs and tasks that many people did in Salem in the 17th century.

2) Better-off villagers like the Putnams may have worn slightly fancier clothes. Although they were still restricted by the Puritan dress code, they may have had some small items of clothing made from expensive materials like lace or silk. They may also have worn buckles on their shoes and hats.

Colour

1) Most clothes would've had muted tones, such as brown and beige.

2) Black dyes were expensive, so black clothes would only have been worn by people with high status.

Fit

The Puritans, particularly the women, were expected to be modest. Women's arms had to be hidden and their skirts had to cover their legs and ankles.

Style

1) Puritan men and women wore modest, simple clothing.

2) Women would typically have worn buttoned blouses, aprons, and long dresses and skirts.

3) Most men would have worn doublets (tight, long-sleeved jackets), knee-length breeches and stockings. Higher status men may have worn tall, wide-brimmed hats.

4) Both men and women would have worn over-sized collars and plain shoes or boots, as well as heavy cloaks or overcoats in colder seasons.

5) Women's hair would've been tied back under a bonnet and they wouldn't have worn make-up.

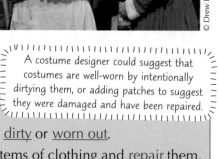
© Drew Farrell/Royal Lyceum Theatre

A costume designer could suggest that costumes are well-worn by intentionally dirtying them, or adding patches to suggest they were damaged and have been repaired.

Condition

1) In a poor farming community like Salem, a lot of people would've had tough, manual jobs, so their clothes would often be dirty or worn out.

2) Puritans didn't have lots of clothes, so they would often wear out items of clothing and repair them.

Costumes can be non-naturalistic too

Designers also need to think about the practicalities of their costumes, including allowing easy movement on stage and quick costume changes.

1) In a non-naturalistic production designers have more freedom, but they still need to consider the effects of their costume choices on the audience.

2) Non-naturalistic costumes are often used to symbolise important aspects of a character (see p.59). They can also be used to highlight the play's themes for the audience.

3) For example, a 2014 production used plain clothing that didn't suggest any particular historical period. This might have been to show that the themes of the play are universal.

Costume

Costume can show basic information about a character...

1) Costumes enable the audience to pinpoint the play's context, identify an actor's character and find out key information about that character.

2) In a naturalistic production, it should be clear from their costumes that Reverend Parris and Reverend Hale are ministers. This could be done using a black cassock (robe) or a square white collar.

A realistic costume can also help a performer to get into character.

3) Hair and make-up can be used to highlight a character's age. For example, older characters like Giles and Rebecca may have grey hair, and a designer could choose to use latex wrinkles on their faces.

4) A character's status can also be shown through costume. As a slave, Tituba has a lower status than the other characters in the play. A costume designer may show this by having Tituba wear a simple smock and walking barefoot throughout the performance.

Effect on the Audience

Miller's stage directions call Abigail "*strikingly beautiful*", whereas Elizabeth describes herself as "plain". To help create this contrast between them for the audience, a make-up artist may highlight Abigail's natural beauty with rosy blusher and mascara to enhance her eyes, whilst giving Elizabeth no obvious make-up.

... and it can also reveal things about their personality

1) To highlight Parris's materialistic side, a costume designer may have the actor wear expensive jewellery or a cassock with golden lace and golden buttons, despite jewellery and expensive materials being generally frowned upon by Puritans.

2) Giving Hale a simpler, unadorned costume would create a contrast between the two ministers and signify to the audience that Hale is more devout and more serious about his profession than Parris.

3) Hair can also show things about a character's personality. Abigail is a confident and spirited character — this could be reflected in her costume by her having long, bouncy, loose hair.

4) To create a contrast between Abigail's and Elizabeth's personalities, a designer might choose to have Elizabeth's hair tightly tied back and covered by a simple white bonnet. This would reflect her more humble nature and the way that she obeys the Puritan dress code.

In this 2017 production, Abigail had free-flowing hair to mirror her rebellious personality.

Costume can have a symbolic meaning

1) A costume designer may choose to symbolise something about a character through a piece of clothing or an aspect of costume. In a non-naturalistic production, Proctor may wear a white shirt with a black stain on his chest, near his heart. Choosing to do this would symbolise the negative effect his affair has had, and the way that it's had a lasting impact.

2) Sometimes, one aspect of costume can signify the whole character. For example, Abigail's rebellious nature might be symbolised by a brightly coloured handkerchief in her pocket or a half-hidden bow in her hair. This would suggest to the audience that she isn't afraid to break the rules.

3) The actor playing Danforth could wear shoes fitted with tap plates to increase the noise he makes when walking around the stage. This would symbolise his authority and his sense of self-importance.

Section Four — Staging and Design

Costume

Costume can be used to support the play's action

A director can use costume to <u>show things</u> to the audience about what's <u>been</u> happening in the play:

- Before the start of Act Two, Proctor has been <u>working in the fields</u>. This could be shown by an actor coming on stage with a <u>dirty</u> and <u>sweaty</u> face and then <u>wiping off</u> this make-up.
- Giles Corey <u>rushes</u> to the Proctors' house after his wife's arrest. His <u>panic</u> and <u>urgency</u> could be reflected to the audience by him <u>not wearing</u> a <u>hat</u> or a <u>coat</u>, even though he's out at <u>night</u>.
- When Francis Nurse enters in Act Two and reveals that Rebecca (his wife) has been arrested, make-up could be used to make his face look <u>flushed</u>. This would help to show how <u>angry</u> and <u>agitated</u> he is.

Change in costume reflects a change in character

The costume designer needs to take into account the way that characters <u>change</u> during the play.

1) In Act Four, Proctor could be wearing <u>tattered rags</u> and have a <u>bloodied</u> face to suggest he's been <u>tortured</u>. He may also have <u>long</u>, <u>unkempt hair</u> to suggest he's been in <u>jail</u> for a <u>long time</u>.

© CATHERINE ASHMORE

2) Elizabeth's clothes may be <u>dirtier</u> in Act Four, and her hair may be <u>untidy</u> and <u>not tied back</u> to show the effects of being in prison.

3) Reverend Hale <u>loses</u> his <u>composure</u> as the play progresses — this could be reflected by his <u>hair</u> becoming <u>messy</u> and his face being dirty. A make-up artist could also draw <u>black shadows</u> under his <u>eyes</u> to suggest that he's been <u>losing sleep</u> over his role in the trials.

4) The actor playing Herrick might be <u>smartly dressed</u> in Act Two and Act Three to show his <u>pride</u> in being a court official. In Act Four, his costume could be <u>dishevelled</u> and <u>unkempt</u> to reflect his drunkenness and to hint that he's <u>ashamed</u> of being associated with the court.

In the exam, think about what costume says about a character

Here's an <u>example</u> of how you could write about <u>Danforth's costume</u>:

> This <u>explains</u> the choice of costume.

I would have Danforth dressed in a long black robe on top of a grey jacket and black trousers, as would be appropriate for an important judge in 17th-century Salem. The black colour would reflect his wealth and status as black dyes were expensive at the time, and having him dressed primarily in black would make him look an imposing and dominant character on stage. I would have his hair a light grey colour to show his age and experience.

> This considers a <u>different aspect</u> of costume.

> This shows the effect on the audience.

I know a costume joke that would have you in stitches...

EXAM TIP

If you get a question about costume design, you need to write about more than just what the characters should wear. Don't forget about hair and make-up, and consider whether costume could be symbolic.

Puppet Design

The Crucible isn't usually performed with puppets, but they could add an extra dimension to a production.

Puppets need to communicate meaning

Puppet design only features on the AQA exam. If you're doing a different exam board, you don't need to read this page. Ask your teacher if you're not sure about this.

1) In a <u>non-naturalistic</u> production, puppets could be used to perform the <u>entire</u> play or they could just be used at <u>key moments</u>.

2) It's a puppet designer's <u>responsibility</u> to think about how puppets could <u>convey meaning</u> to the audience.

3) For example, the <u>size</u> of puppets can show their <u>status</u> and <u>importance</u> to the story. For puppets that represent characters, a designer may use <u>larger</u>, <u>more detailed puppets</u> for <u>main characters</u> like Proctor.

4) As well as size, puppet designers need to think carefully about their use of <u>colour</u> and <u>material</u>. For example, a puppet that represents Abigail may be made from <u>brightly coloured</u>, <u>silken</u> material to reinforce her <u>seductive</u> nature.

Puppets can help the audience interpret the action

A director could use puppets <u>alongside</u> actors. They might do this to give the audience <u>extra information</u>, highlight an <u>important moment</u> or show something that might otherwise be <u>difficult</u> to stage.

SHADOW PUPPETS

- A puppet designer could use <u>shadow puppets</u> behind a <u>gauze screen</u> to show the girls <u>dancing</u> and <u>singing</u> in the forest before Act One. The use of <u>silhouettes</u> would reinforce the idea that their behaviour is both <u>mysterious</u> and <u>forbidden</u>.

- Shadow puppets could also be used before the start of Act Four to show Abigail and Mercy <u>creeping away</u> from Salem. This would suggest that they fled <u>secretively</u>, and the use of <u>black shadows</u> could symbolise how the trials have <u>tainted their reputations</u>.

ROD PUPPETS

- A puppet designer may use a <u>bird puppet</u> in Act Three to show what the girls 'see'. The actor playing Abigail could <u>control</u> the bird puppet using a rod to show how she is <u>manipulating</u> the situation. Since the audience <u>can</u> see the puppet, but a lot of the characters on stage <u>can't</u>, this could symbolise how <u>illusion</u> and <u>reality</u> have become <u>blurred</u> in Salem.

© Donald Cooper/photostage

STRING PUPPETS

- At the end of Act One, Abigail could have puppets with nooses round their necks <u>fall from her fingers</u> as she accuses people. This would show her <u>control</u> of the situation and <u>foreshadow</u> the hangings later in the play.

- A puppet could be <u>strung up</u> at the end of Act Four to show Proctor's <u>death</u>. Using a puppet would allow a director to show this <u>dramatic moment</u> without risking the <u>safety</u> of the actor playing Proctor. The puppet could <u>hang in silence</u> to provide a <u>powerful final image</u> to the audience.

REVISION TASK

I spy a ~~poppet~~ puppet, Goody Proctor...

Choose a scene from the play and consider how you would use a puppet to portray one of the characters in that scene. Write a paragraph that answers the following questions:

1) Why is it suitable to use a puppet for this character?

2) What elements might you consider when designing the puppet?

3) What would the effect be of using a puppet in the scene?

Tick list:
✓ effect of puppets on the audience
✓ making and styling puppets

Practice Questions

Well, that was a bit intense... but it's not quite over yet. Here are some lovely practice questions to make sure you've taken in all that design knowledge. Have a good go at these before you move on to Section Five.

Quick Questions

1) Name two practicalities that a director should consider when choosing a stage type for a production of *The Crucible*.

2) Give two materials that a set designer might use in a naturalistic set design for *The Crucible*.

3) Give one reason why a set designer might use oversized scenery in *The Crucible*.

4) Why might a set designer include technical devices in sets for the play? Give two reasons.

5) Give two examples of how personal props could be used to reinforce characterisation in *The Crucible*.

6) Why might a lighting designer use blue-tinted gels in Act Four?

7) Describe how lighting could be used to create a shadow on stage.

8) Give an example of when a sound designer might use amplification in *The Crucible*.

9) Give five considerations for a costume designer creating naturalistic costumes for the play.

In-depth Questions

1) Explain the design ideas you would use to create an authentic 17th-century Puritan setting in Act Two. Refer to the context of the play in your answer.

2) Choose a stage type and explain why you think it would be appropriate for staging a production of *The Crucible*. Use examples from the play to back up your answer.

3) How might a set designer use colour symbolism in a non-naturalistic production of *The Crucible*? Explain the reasons behind your ideas.

4) How might lighting be used to create a tense atmosphere for the audience just before Elizabeth lies about Proctor's affair in Act Three?

5) What sounds would you include in a soundscape for the jail scene in Act Four? Explain how you would create these sounds.

Practice Questions

After all that hard work thinking and reading about staging and design in the play, you probably can't wait to actually write about it. Luckily for you, there's a whole page of exam-style questions to get stuck into...

Exam-style Questions

Find the part of Act One where the girls are left alone together. Read from where Abigail says "**How is Ruth sick?**" to where she says "**I say shut it, Mary Warren!**", then answer Question 1 below.

1) Imagine you're a designer working on *The Crucible*. Explain how you would use staging and set design to portray this extract effectively on stage to the audience. In your answer, you should refer to the play's context.

Find the part of Act Two where Hale enters the Proctors' house. Read from where Hale says "**Good evening**" to where he says "**Oh, did you! That's a good sign, then**", then answer Question 2 below.

2) Imagine you're a costume designer working on staging this extract of *The Crucible*. Describe how you would use costume design to create effects that reinforce the action in this extract. You should explain why your ideas are suitable for this extract and for the rest of the play.

Find the part of Act Two where Elizabeth has just been arrested. Read from "***Proctor stands there, gulping air***" to the end of the act, then answer Question 3 below.

3) Imagine you are a sound designer working on *The Crucible*. Explain how you would use sound design to stage this extract effectively for the audience.

Read Act Three from where Parris says "**Praise God!**" to the end of the act, then answer Question 4 below.

4) Imagine you're a lighting designer working on staging this extract of *The Crucible*. Describe how you would use lighting design to create effects that reinforce the action in this extract. You should explain why your ideas are suitable for this extract and for the rest of the play.

Act One

This section looks at performance skills and design features using the kind of close analysis you should be doing in the exam — what a treat. If you need a reminder of the plot, flick back to the introduction (p.4-5).

Act One creates a mood of fear and distrust

1) Act One plays an important role in setting the <u>mood</u> and <u>atmosphere</u> of the play — from the moment the play starts, Miller shows the audience that life in <u>Salem</u> is dominated by <u>fear</u> and <u>suspicion</u>.

2) This can be seen in the way the characters <u>interact</u> with one another. Reverend Parris interrogates his own niece (Abigail), which immediately introduces an atmosphere of <u>distrust</u>. His <u>anxiety</u> about Betty and <u>anger</u> at Abigail show that he's <u>afraid</u> of the impact that their actions could have on his <u>reputation</u>.

3) The atmosphere of <u>fear</u> is developed even more when Abigail <u>threatens</u> Mary, Mercy and Betty. This shows that Abigail is in charge, but it also suggests that she <u>fears the consequences</u> of being accused of <u>witchcraft</u>. Her threats <u>foreshadow</u> the more <u>serious accusations</u> that she makes about Tituba <u>later in the act</u>.

© Drew Farrell/Royal Lyceum Theatre

4) Hale's interrogation of Tituba <u>maintains</u> the atmosphere of fear and distrust — she's <u>scared</u> into <u>confessing</u> to <u>witchcraft</u> by the threat of execution, before being <u>pressured</u> into accusing other villagers of the same thing. This creates an <u>unsettling mood</u> for the audience, as they <u>don't know</u> which characters they can <u>trust</u>.

Parris questions Abigail over what happened in the forest

1) Reverend Parris reveals his <u>anxiety</u> and <u>suspicion</u> when he <u>interrogates</u> Abigail. The actors playing Parris and Abigail could use <u>physical skills</u> to enhance the impact of this exchange on the audience:

Physical Skills — Movement

*   An actor playing Parris could <u>pace up and down</u> the stage <u>frantically</u> to show that he's anxious about the villagers' reaction to Abigail's behaviour. He might also <u>approach</u> Abigail and <u>stare</u> at her with a <u>narrow gaze</u> when she's speaking, as if he's trying to decide whether or not she's telling the <u>truth</u>.

*   An actor playing Abigail might remain <u>still</u> while she defends herself. This would provide a <u>contrast</u> to Parris's <u>erratic movements</u> and suggest that she feels <u>more composed</u> than him. Her stillness could also suggest that she's trying to earn Parris's trust by making herself appear <u>obedient</u> and <u>innocent</u>.

*   When Parris mentions Elizabeth Proctor, Abigail might suddenly <u>spring into life</u> — an actor could use <u>animated gestures</u> to show that she can't contain her <u>hatred</u> for her. This would give the audience the sense that they're seeing the '<u>real</u>' Abigail, which might suggest that Parris is <u>right</u> not to <u>trust</u> her.

2) At this point in Act One, the audience are forming their <u>first impressions</u> of the characters. The actors' <u>costumes</u> are just as important as their <u>physical performance</u> in shaping the audience's <u>initial reaction</u>:

Costume Design — Clothing

*   As a Puritan minister, Parris would be expected to <u>dress neatly</u>, but in this act he might have an <u>open collar</u> and <u>untucked shirt</u>. This would make him look <u>untidy</u>, suggesting he's been <u>worrying all night</u>.

*   Abigail could wear a <u>plain costume</u> to reflect her Puritan upbringing, but <u>small details</u> might be <u>added</u> to reveal more about her <u>character</u>. For example, a <u>red ribbon</u> could be tied to her bonnet. This <u>colour symbolism</u> (see p.52) would hint at Abigail's <u>passionate</u> nature and suggest that she's hiding a <u>rebellious</u> side from Parris.

*   Betty remains <u>motionless</u> on the bed at this point, but her costume is still <u>important</u>. An actor might be wearing a <u>simple</u>, <u>white nightgown</u> to emphasise her <u>vulnerability and innocence</u> to the audience.

Act One

Abigail threatens Mary, Mercy and Betty

1) When Abigail warns the other girls not to admit to dancing in the woods, there's an atmosphere of fear and danger. Lighting could be used to focus the audience's attention on the girls' anxiety.

2) The stage directions say that "*morning sunlight*" is streaming through the window of Parris's house. The stage could be gently lit from the front using a floodlight to give an impression of natural light.

Physical Skills — Body Language

- An actor playing Abigail could stand tall and march purposefully towards Mary and Mercy to appear threatening — this body language would demonstrate her authority over them.

- The other girls might adopt a slightly hunched posture and shy away from Abigail to further highlight her physical dominance.

- Abigail "*furiously shakes*" Betty and "*smashes her across the face*". These actions might be exaggerated, as if Abigail is using excessive force. This would shock the audience.

3) When Abigail threatens the other girls, this lighting could slowly become harsher and less natural until the whole stage is brightly lit up. This would create an unsettling effect and reflect the emotional intensity of this moment.

4) A profile spotlight might cast a sharply-defined beam on Mary and Mercy when Abigail begins to threaten them. This could communicate the intense pressure they're feeling to the audience, especially if the light was shone into their faces.

5) When Abigail says her speech beginning "Now look you", a narrow beam of light could be shone on her from directly above to mark her out as the dominant figure on stage. This would also cast highly unusual shadows on her face and body, giving her a threatening appearance.

Tituba cracks under extreme pressure

1) When Tituba is interrogated, an actor could use a wide range of vocal performance skills to show her emotional turmoil.

2) Tituba might respond to Reverend Hale's initial accusations quickly, forcefully and in a confident tone — "I don't truck with no Devil!" This would show her fear of being blamed unfairly, but also her absolute certainty that she's innocent.

3) However, Tituba's speech could slow down later on to show that she's losing confidence. This would emphasise a lack of conviction in her words, as though she's only saying what she believes the other characters want to hear.

4) She confesses to witchcraft after Putnam threatens her with hanging. When she says "No, no, don't hang Tituba!", she might speak loudly and at a higher pitch. This would show that she's terrified by this threat.

5) When Tituba gets carried away and accuses other villagers, an actor might pause for a long time between saying "I look —" and revealing the first name ("and there was Goody Good"). This would suggest that Tituba knows it's wrong to accuse these villagers, but does it out of desperation to save her own life.

© KS-Fotografie/action press/REX/Shutterstock

In this production, the actor playing Tituba sobs on her knees to clearly show her distress.

Effect on the Audience

The audience is more likely to sympathise with Tituba if they believe that she's innocent. The actor might fidget agitatedly and cry out to suggest that stress and fear cause her to make a false confession.

EXAM TIP

Think about atmosphere, even if you're not in the mood...

The decisions made by the director, actors or designers have an impact on the mood and atmosphere on stage. Consider the overall effect you want to create before settling on any performance or design ideas.

Act Two

A week has passed and the witch trials have started. It's not the best time to be having marital issues, but that's exactly what the Proctors are going through — sounds like a chance for some more close analysis...

Act Two focuses on the Proctors

1) Act Two gives the audience an insight into the <u>relationship</u> between <u>Proctor</u> and <u>Elizabeth</u>. There's <u>tension</u> between them as a result of Proctor's <u>affair</u>, but they still care about each other — Proctor becomes <u>protective</u> over Elizabeth when the witch trials <u>threaten</u> her <u>safety</u>.

2) Elizabeth is <u>mentioned</u> by Proctor and Abigail in Act One, but this is the <u>first time</u> she appears <u>on stage</u>. The audience gets a <u>brief glimpse</u> of how she feels about Proctor's <u>affair</u> during her conversation with him, but it's interrupted when Mary tells her that she's been accused of <u>witchcraft</u>. Elizabeth's <u>reaction</u> to the <u>bad news</u> reveals more about her <u>character</u>.

Take a look at p.28-33 for more suggestions on how an actor could play Proctor or Elizabeth.

3) Proctor's behaviour is just as <u>revealing</u>. Hale challenges him to recite the <u>Ten Commandments</u> as a test of his family's "<u>Christian character</u>", but he <u>can't</u> — the <u>anxiety</u> that this causes him shows his fear that his <u>less strict approach</u> to religion could get him and Elizabeth into <u>trouble</u>.

4) There's <u>nothing</u> Proctor can do to <u>prevent</u> Elizabeth from being <u>arrested</u>. The audience now knows that Proctor <u>cares</u> for Elizabeth, which makes their separation <u>more dramatic</u>.

Elizabeth finds out that she's been accused

1) Elizabeth is <u>cautious</u> about showing any <u>emotion</u> to Proctor at the start of the act, but she becomes less guarded when Mary returns from Salem and says that Elizabeth has been accused of <u>witchcraft</u>. Here, an actor could use <u>vocal skills</u> to express Elizabeth's <u>emotions</u> to the audience.

2) The stage directions say that Elizabeth speaks "*softly*" and "*quietly*" after finding out about the accusation. This would suggest that she's <u>stunned</u> and <u>doesn't know</u> how to <u>respond</u>. She might speak <u>slowly</u> and <u>deliberately</u>, as if she's trying to <u>stay in control</u> of her emotions.

3) However, her speech might rapidly <u>increase in volume</u> as she realises that <u>Abigail</u> must have been the one to accuse her — "She wants me dead, John, you know it!" This <u>emotional outburst</u> would suggest that her <u>deep-set hatred</u> for Abigail has caused her to <u>lose her composure</u>, especially if an actor playing Elizabeth almost <u>spits out</u> the word "<u>she</u>".

4) Elizabeth's interaction with Proctor can be used to show her <u>mistrust</u>. When she tells Proctor that Abigail has an "arrow" in him, she expresses <u>concern</u> that he might still be attracted to Abigail. At this moment, her voice might <u>tremble</u> slightly, showing she is worried that Proctor is unwilling to go to Abigail to get her to drop the charges. This would suggest that she has <u>lost faith</u> in him as a result of his <u>affair</u>.

Design — Staging

- In this part of Act Two, the choice of <u>staging</u> will have a <u>major impact</u> on the audience's experience of the action. For example, staging the play <u>in the round</u> (see p.46) would create a <u>claustrophobic atmosphere</u>, which might give the audience a sense that Elizabeth feels <u>trapped</u> by the <u>accusations</u>.

- On an end-on stage, the <u>door</u> to the Proctors' house could be placed in a <u>prominent downstage position</u> so that <u>Mary's entrance</u> is <u>more noticeable</u>. The <u>staircase</u> could be <u>upstage</u> so her <u>exit</u> is <u>less obvious</u> to the audience, allowing them to <u>concentrate</u> on Proctor and Elizabeth's reactions to her news.

- A <u>large performance space</u> would help to highlight the <u>distance</u> between the Proctors before Elizabeth is accused. After Elizabeth learns of the accusation, Proctor could <u>move across the stage</u> to join her, as if he wants to <u>protect</u> her — this movement would be <u>clearer</u> and <u>more effective</u> in a <u>larger space</u>.

Act Two

Proctor recites the Ten Commandments

1) Proctor is <u>caught off guard</u> by the news that Elizabeth has been accused — he's "*still in his shock*" when Reverend Hale arrives unannounced. When Proctor is told to recite the <u>Ten Commandments</u>, an actor could use <u>physical skills</u> to show how <u>anxious</u> he is to prove that he and his wife are <u>devout</u> Christians.

This actor playing Proctor positions himself protectively in front of Elizabeth.

2) An actor might <u>wipe his brow</u> to suggest that Proctor has become <u>flushed</u> when Hale asks "Let you repeat them". This would show that he knows how <u>important</u> it is to <u>prove</u> Elizabeth's <u>innocence</u> at this moment, and that he's feeling a lot of <u>pressure</u> as a result.

3) He might also <u>shift his weight</u> from <u>one foot</u> to the <u>other</u> while speaking. This would imply that Proctor feels <u>uneasy</u> because he <u>isn't confident</u> about remembering them <u>all</u>. An actor could also create this effect by <u>glancing nervously</u> around the room for help.

4) The stage directions indicate that Proctor <u>grins</u> to make light of his <u>forgetfulness</u> in an attempt to make Hale <u>less suspicious</u> of him and Elizabeth. An actor might <u>lean back</u> in a <u>casual stance</u> as he smiles, as if Proctor wants to <u>downplay</u> the importance of missing out one Commandment ("I think it be a small fault").

Effect on the Audience

<u>Proctor</u> hasn't been accused of anything yet — it's <u>Elizabeth</u> that he's worried about. The more an actor brings out Proctor's <u>concern</u>, the more it will seem like he <u>loves</u> and <u>cares</u> for his wife.

Elizabeth is arrested by Ezekiel Cheever

1) Proctor's concern for Elizabeth's safety seems justified when Cheever comes to <u>arrest</u> her. This is already a <u>tense moment</u>, but its impact on the audience can be <u>enhanced</u> through the appropriate use of <u>sound</u>.

2) There is a "<u>*shocked silence*</u>" when Cheever arrives — this stage direction applies to the actors, but the <u>sound effects</u> might be <u>cut off</u> at the <u>same time</u>. This <u>silence</u> would stress the <u>importance</u> of this moment to the audience, as well as drawing attention to how <u>surprised</u> the characters are by Cheever's <u>entrance</u>.

3) Proctor and Elizabeth's voices could be <u>amplified differently</u> to stress their <u>differing reactions</u> to the arrest. Proctor's voice might be louder to show his <u>anger</u> and <u>guilt</u>, but Elizabeth's might be <u>barely audible</u> to show that she's <u>quietly accepting</u> of her <u>fate</u>.

4) The dialogue might also be accompanied by a range of <u>diegetic sounds</u> (see p.55). Some actors could talk <u>offstage</u> to suggest that people are waiting <u>outside</u> to take Elizabeth, and the <u>sound of chains</u> could be heard once after she has exited the stage. This would highlight that Proctor is <u>powerless</u> to intervene in his wife's arrest.

Design — Props

- Cheever brandishes a <u>warrant</u> to show that he has the authority of the court. It might have an <u>official red seal</u> to make it seem <u>important</u> — this would make it <u>more shocking</u> when Proctor <u>rips</u> it.

- Elizabeth is <u>incriminated</u> by a <u>poppet</u> which is found on the fireplace. Placing this prop in an <u>obvious position</u> would add to the <u>tension</u> when she claims to have "<u>no poppets</u>" — the audience would have already seen the poppet, so they would know that she might be <u>found out</u>.

The 11th Commandment — thou shalt not be too vague...

It's important to use relevant details when explaining your ideas in the exam. Even small details like a facial expression or a well-placed prop can affect the audience's experience of the play in a big way.

Act Three

If you thought Act Two was dramatic, just wait until you feast your eyes on Act Three. Proctor descends on the Salem meeting house to rescue Elizabeth, but nothing seems to go his way — let's take a closer look...

Act Three ramps up the tension and pace

1) Act Three rapidly increases the tension and the pace of the action by developing the conflict between opposing characters. The act eventually reaches a dramatic climax, where the tension is at its highest.

2) Mary's admission that she was lying about seeing spirits is a crucial moment in the creation of tension. The audience isn't sure whether or not she'll have the courage to confess to the judges, and they don't know whether she'll stand by her confession for the whole act. This doubt creates a tense atmosphere.

3) The judges decide to question Mary, Abigail and the other girls again. The pace accelerates as the characters argue amongst themselves, and the climax arrives when Proctor is forced to admit to adultery in order to discredit Abigail.

4) This high level of tension is sustained until the end of the act, when Mary has a sudden change of heart and calls Proctor "the Devil's man". This false accusation creates suspense for the audience — they can only look on as Proctor is arrested for witchcraft.

> **Effect on the Audience**
>
> In Act Three, the audience is likely to feel sorry for Proctor (the protagonist), but condemn Abigail (the antagonist). It's not clear who the judges will believe, which creates tension for the audience as they wait for the outcome of Proctor and Abigail's conflict.

Mary admits that she was lying in court

1) Mary only has a few lines when she first confesses to lying, but an actor can still use her vocal skills to give the audience an insight into her thoughts and feelings. For example, she might use a low, soft voice to confess that her earlier testimony was just "pretence". This would show that she's frightened and reluctant to speak up.

2) When Danforth interrogates Mary about her confession, she repeats "I am with God" to convince him that she's honest. An actor could deliver this line hastily and without intonation, as if she's only saying it to put an end to Danforth's questioning.

3) An actor could stutter or stumble over her words to show that Mary is intimidated by Danforth. This would create tension by suggesting that Mary might crack under the pressure of his questioning — the audience knows that Proctor and Elizabeth will be in trouble if she does.

> **Costume Design — Hair and Make-Up**
>
> - At this moment in the play, the costume designer could use hair and make-up to give the audience an insight into Mary's state of mind. For example, Mary might have red, puffy eyes to show that she was crying just before she entered the courtroom.
> - The rest of Mary's face could be covered in pale make-up to make it seem like her face is drained of colour. This would imply that she's frightened to admit that she was lying in front of the judges.
> - Mary's hair could be pulled back under a bonnet — a typical look for 17th-century Puritan women. However, small strands of hair might be sticking out to suggest that it was done carelessly. This would make it seem like Mary is in a fragile mental state.

See p.59 for more on hair and make-up design.

© Felicity Peacock/ Oxford Theatre Guild

Act Three

Proctor confesses to adultery

1) When the judges are listening to Proctor and the girls, <u>lighting</u> could be used to create tension. Stage lights could be used to make the judges' reactions <u>clearly visible</u>. A <u>broad wash</u> of <u>front lighting</u> would allow the audience to <u>read</u> their <u>facial expressions</u> and <u>guess</u> whether they'll rule in Proctor's favour.

2) In a <u>non-naturalistic</u> production, when Proctor "*leaps*" at Abigail and grabs her by the hair, <u>red-tinted gels</u> could be placed over the stage lanterns to cast <u>red light</u> across the stage. This <u>unnatural</u> lighting would reflect Proctor's <u>anger</u> through <u>colour symbolism</u>, as well as increasing the <u>intensity</u> of the moment.

3) The lighting could <u>fade</u> while Proctor confesses to adultery until he alone is lit up by a <u>profile spotlight</u>. This would draw the audience's attention towards Proctor and highlight the <u>importance</u> of his <u>confession</u>.

© Alastair Muir/REX/Shutterstock

This actor's fierce facial expression reflects Proctor's momentary loss of control.

Physical Skills — Movement

- After Mary fails to faint, Proctor's <u>movements</u> might become gradually more <u>agitated</u>. This would make him seem <u>increasingly concerned</u> that the judges <u>won't believe</u> him.
- When Proctor realises that he has <u>no choice</u> but to admit to <u>adultery</u>, he briefly <u>loses control</u>. An actor might use <u>sudden</u> and <u>rapid movements</u> when rushing at Abigail to reflect this.
- However, Proctor might stand <u>motionless</u> after regaining his <u>composure</u> and saying "I have known her". This stillness would suggest that he's <u>suddenly</u> overcome with <u>guilt</u>.

Mary accuses Proctor of witchcraft

1) At the end of the act, Mary is <u>torn</u> between <u>telling the truth</u> and <u>saving herself</u>. An actor could stand at <u>centre stage</u>, equally far apart from Proctor and the girls — this use of <u>proxemics</u> would stress Mary's <u>dilemma</u> by presenting it to the audience <u>visually</u>.

2) Mary decides to side with the <u>girls</u> and accuse <u>Proctor</u> instead. At this point, an actor could <u>move closer</u> to the girls to show that she has made up her mind. She could even <u>cower behind</u> the girls to suggest that she's <u>scared</u> of Proctor.

Effect on the Audience

The play's <u>climax</u> happens earlier in Act Three, but it doesn't put an end to the <u>suspense</u>. Mary's <u>accusation</u> creates <u>uncertainty</u> in the audience about what will happen to Proctor.

3) Proxemics could also be used to show what the <u>other characters</u> are thinking. Danforth and Parris might stand nearer to the <u>girls</u>, whereas Hale might stand closer to <u>Proctor</u> when he says "Excellency, this child's gone wild!" This would show that Hale's the <u>only</u> one of the three who <u>doesn't believe</u> Mary.

Sound Design — Music

- Miller <u>doesn't</u> include any <u>stage directions</u> for <u>live music</u>, but it could be added for <u>dramatic effect</u> at this point. For example, <u>frantic, high-pitched violin music</u> might start to play when the girls pretend to have visions of a "yellow bird". This music would <u>mimic</u> the <u>uncontrolled nature</u> of their <u>outbursts</u>.
- The music might <u>continue</u> after Mary accuses Proctor of witchcraft, but it could become <u>quieter</u> and <u>more sombre</u>. This would suggest that Mary's accusations will have <u>tragic consequences</u> for Proctor.

EXAM TIP

I dunno about you, but I can't tell which witch is which...

Act Three is pretty chaotic, so remember to keep your exam response focused on the question you've been asked. Being consistent should help — the decisions you choose should all work well together.

Act Four

The Crucible is a tragedy, so unfortunately there's no happy ending. Proctor's stay in Salem prison is about to take a miserable turn — there are just a few important moments to analyse before he meets his maker.

Act Four brings the play to a tragic conclusion

© Felicity Peacock/ Oxford Theatre Guild

1) Act Four ties up loose ends in the plot and brings the action to a tragic conclusion. Miller offers the audience a glimmer of hope that Proctor's life will be spared, but he snatches it away again at the end of the play.

2) The first moment that contributes to the tragic ending occurs when Hale and Danforth plead with Elizabeth to get Proctor to confess to witchcraft. She refuses, but this moment raises the possibility that Proctor might live — this suggests his death was avoidable, which makes it seem more tragic.

3) Proctor and Elizabeth are allowed to speak privately, but Elizabeth won't influence Proctor's decision. Watching him agonise over whether or not to confess highlights the tragedy of his situation — imprisonment and death are the only possible outcomes, so there's no chance of a happy ending.

4) Proctor decides to sign the confession, but he's overwhelmed by guilt. There's a strong sense of tragedy when he tears it in front of the judges, as the audience knows that he has condemned himself to death.

Hale and Danforth plead with Elizabeth

1) The whole of Act Four takes place in a prison cell. The set design should reflect the bleakness of this setting. This would create a dark atmosphere that hints at the tragedy to follow.

Set Design — Scenery

- Miller's stage directions say that the cell has a "*high barred window*" and a "*heavy door*", along with "*two benches*". This suggests that it's a bare room with few props or items of furniture.
- However, the set designer can use the scenery to produce a gloomy effect. Grey lines could be painted on a flat of the cell window to represent iron bars, and the door could be made to look like solid oak. These materials are strong, so they would emphasise it's impossible for Proctor to escape.
- The walls and floor of the cell could be made to look like dull, grey stone material. This would make the cell seem dark and confined, adding further to the claustrophobic atmosphere. The floor might be strewn with straw and dirt to highlight the uncomfortable conditions in prison.

2) Hale and Danforth want Proctor to confess, but for different reasons — Hale doesn't want Proctor to die, while Danforth wants to use his confession to justify hanging other prisoners. When they're asking Elizabeth for help, the actors can use vocal skills to show the difference in their approaches:

Vocal Skills — Hale

- Hale might start speaking to Elizabeth in a calm, soothing tone when he says "I would save your husband's life". This would show that he's genuinely concerned for Proctor.
- However, he quickly becomes frustrated by Elizabeth's stubbornness — when he shouts "Woman, before the laws of God we are as swine!", the actor might emphasise the first and last words. This would suggest that he's desperate for Elizabeth to change her mind.

Vocal Skills — Danforth

- Danforth isn't used to pleading with others, so he might use a dismissive tone when he asks Hale to speak to Elizabeth for him — "Mr Hale, will you speak with the woman?"
- When Hale fails to get through to Elizabeth, Danforth intervenes. He might speak more forcefully, as though it's the only way she'll understand — "He will die with the sunrise. Your husband." This may also make it seem like he doesn't care if Proctor lives or dies.

Act Four

Proctor and Elizabeth speak privately

1) When Proctor enters the prison cell, the stage directions describe him as "_another man_" — a costume designer could take this chance to show how much Proctor has changed in prison.

2) Proctor's skin and hair could be covered in filth. His grimy appearance could increase the audience's sympathy for him, especially if he was clean and well-groomed earlier on in the play.

3) Proctor's costume might include a threadbare shirt and trousers in a faded dark brown colour, and he might have bare feet. This would imply that he's worn the same clothes for weeks, which might attract even more sympathy from the audience.

4) These clothes might be loose-fitting, as a way of showing the audience that he has lost weight.

Physical Skills — Facial Expressions

- Elizabeth's facial expressions could be used to indicate how she's feeling when she's speaking to Proctor. For example, an actor might use a weary expression to imply that she's physically and emotionally drained from being in prison.

- Elizabeth refuses to tell Proctor whether or not he should confess. She may avoid eye contact when she says "As you will, I would have it" so that she doesn't give away her thoughts to him.

- At the end of the conversation, she might look like she's holding back tears. This would show that she knows there's no chance of a positive outcome — Proctor will either die, or survive and be damned for making a false confession.

Proctor tears his confession to shreds

1) There's a sudden change in Proctor's behaviour at the end of Act Four — one moment he's signing the confession, but the next he's tearing it up. This requires the actor to change his physical performance.

2) When Proctor is preparing to sign the confession, the actor's body language might hint at how guilty he feels for lying to save his own life. He might slump his shoulders or bow his head to express his shame.

© Geraint Lewis / Alamy Stock Photo

3) Proctor is so ashamed of himself that he "_turns his face to the wall_" to avoid looking at Rebecca Nurse. At this moment, he may also close his eyes to avoid eye contact with anyone else.

4) However, Proctor doesn't stick to his confession for very long. He might wave the confession wildly in Danforth's face when he says "You have no need for this" to reflect the "_wild terror_" that he's feeling during this moment.

5) Although Proctor is "_weeping in fury_" when he tears the confession, the actor might stand up tall, as if telling the truth has lifted a weight off his shoulders. It's a brave decision by Proctor, but the audience knows that he'll be hanged for it — this makes it a deeply tragic moment from their point of view.

Effect on the Audience

Catharsis occurs when the tragic events of a play cause the audience to feel and release strong emotions of their own. To create this effect, the actor playing Proctor could combine physical skills and vocal skills in a way that reflects his emotional turmoil. This would make the play's final moments much more dramatic to watch, and would provide a sense of conclusion for the audience by allowing a moment of release for their own emotions.

EXAM TIP

Death or damnation — talk about a lose-lose situation...

Some moments are trickier to direct, perform and design than others. There's no right or wrong way of tackling them, so don't be afraid to get creative — just remember to stick to the style of the production.

Practice Questions

You're probably ready for a breather after all of that close analysis, but don't reach for the TV remote just yet — you'll enjoy that episode of 'Salem's Got Talent' much more if you get these questions out of the way first.

Quick Questions

1) What kind of atmosphere might a director try to create in Act One?

2) What effect would be created if an actor playing Abigail used animated movements after Parris mentions Elizabeth in Act One?

3) Why might a lighting designer choose to cast a shadow on Abigail when she threatens the other girls in Act One?

4) Give one way that an actor playing Elizabeth might use vocal skills to show hatred for Abigail in Act Two.

5) Why would staging the play in the round enhance the idea that Elizabeth can't escape the accusations in Act Two?

6) How might an actor emphasise Proctor's anxiety after Elizabeth is accused in Act Two?

7) Give one way that an actor playing Mary might use vocal skills to show that she's intimidated in Act Three.

8) In Act Three, why is it important for the judges' faces to be clearly visible?

9) How might a set designer create a bleak setting in Act Four?

In-depth Questions

1) Describe a costume design for Proctor in Act One, then explain how this costume would change in Act Four. Explain the effect of these changes on the audience.

2) Explain how the actors playing Proctor and Elizabeth might use physical skills to highlight their differing reactions to Elizabeth's arrest. What would this reveal about their characters?

3) Explain three ways in which you would use music and sound effects to create a tense atmosphere at the beginning of Act Three.

4) How could set design be used to help create an oppressive atmosphere when Danforth questions Abigail in Act Three?

5) Choose a moment from Act Four. Explain how proxemics could be used to reveal more about the relationships between the characters at this moment.

Practice Questions

If you don't know 'The Crucible' inside out by now, I'll eat my pointy hat. This section is packed full of the kind of detailed analysis that will impress the examiners on the day — practise using the same level of detail when you answer the exam-style questions below. That way, including it in the exam will be a doddle...

Exam-style Questions

> Find the part of Act One where Abigail is talking alone with Reverend Parris. Read from where Abigail says "**I would never hurt Betty**" to where she says "**Goody Proctor is a gossiping liar!**", then answer Questions 1 and 2 below.

1) Imagine you're a performer playing Abigail. Discuss how you would use your performance skills to portray her in this extract. You should explain why your ideas are suitable for this extract and for the rest of the play.

2) Imagine you're a lighting designer working on a production of the play. Describe how you would use lighting design to create effects that reinforce the action in this extract. You should explain why your ideas are suitable for this extract and for the rest of the play.

> Find the part of Act Three where the girls pretend to see the yellow bird. Read from where Mary says "**Abby, stop it!**" to where she says "**Don't touch me — don't touch me!**", then answer Questions 3-5 below.

3) Reread the extract, from the start of the passage to where Proctor says "**They're gulling you, Mister!**" Imagine you're a performer playing Mary. Explain how you and the performers playing the girls might use the space on stage and interact together to create tension for the audience in this part of the extract.

4) Find the line where Proctor says "**God damns liars, Mary!**" Imagine you're a performer playing Proctor. Describe how you would perform this line using your vocal and physical skills. You should explain the effects you want to create.

5) Imagine you're a set designer working on *The Crucible*. Explain how you would use special effects to stage this extract effectively for the audience.

About the Exam

This section will help you to prepare for the part of your exam that will test you on your understanding of *The Crucible*. Yep, it's all starting to feel pretty real now, so you'd best take a deep breath and get cracking...

'The Crucible' will be assessed in a written exam

1) One section of your exam will require you to answer questions on *The Crucible*. These questions might focus on an <u>extract</u> from the play, or they might ask about an extract <u>and</u> the <u>play as a whole</u>.

2) For this part of the exam, you'll be <u>assessed</u> on your <u>knowledge</u> of <u>how</u> the play could be <u>developed</u> and <u>performed</u>.

3) There will be both <u>short and long questions</u>. Manage your <u>time carefully</u> so you have <u>plenty of time</u> to answer the longer questions — if a question is worth <u>twice the marks</u> of another, you should spend <u>twice as long</u> on it.

If you're sitting the AQA exam, you may get a choice of questions — make sure you read the exam paper carefully and answer the right number of questions.

You'll answer from different perspectives

1) The questions could ask you to write from the perspective of a <u>performer</u>, <u>designer</u> or <u>director</u>:

- As a **PERFORMER**, you'll need to think about how you would use your performance skills to portray a certain <u>character</u>. This could include <u>physical skills</u> and <u>vocal skills</u>.
- As a **DESIGNER**, you'll need to come up with <u>design ideas</u> that would enhance the impact of a <u>play</u>. This requires a good <u>understanding</u> of design elements like <u>set</u>, <u>lighting</u> and <u>sound</u>.
- As a **DIRECTOR**, you'll need to consider how you would bring a <u>written text</u> to life <u>on stage</u>. You'll be asked to focus on <u>one element</u> of the <u>production</u> in your answer.

2) Some questions might <u>give you</u> an aspect of production or design to write about, or you might get to <u>choose</u>. You could also be given <u>options</u> — e.g. you might need to focus on either <u>set</u>, <u>lighting</u> or <u>sound</u>.

3) You <u>can't</u> just learn about the roles and responsibilities of <u>one type</u> of theatre maker — over the course of the written exam, you might be expected to answer from <u>all three perspectives</u>.

You'll always need to write about certain aspects

1) No matter which perspective you're writing from, there are some <u>general points</u> you'll need to <u>consider</u>:

- Miller's <u>intentions</u> and what he wants to convey — <u>stage directions</u> are useful for this.
- How the play's <u>historical</u>, <u>social</u>, <u>cultural</u> and <u>theatrical contexts</u> might <u>affect</u> a production.
- The <u>roles</u> and <u>responsibilities</u> of <u>theatre makers</u> and how they bring the play to life, as well as any <u>challenges</u> they may face.
- The <u>genres</u> and <u>style</u> of the play. You should explore how these can be <u>conveyed</u> to the <u>audience</u>.

2) To get <u>top marks</u> in the exam, you should <u>also</u>:

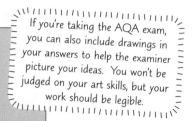

If you're taking the AQA exam, you can also include drawings in your answers to help the examiner picture your ideas. You won't be judged on your art skills, but your work should be legible.

- Use accurate <u>technical language</u> when describing aspects of <u>performance skills</u>, <u>design features</u> and <u>stage configurations</u>.
- Use <u>examples</u> (e.g. <u>quotes</u>, <u>context</u> or <u>events</u>) that demonstrate <u>understanding</u> of the play and <u>support</u> the point you're making.
- Give <u>specific</u>, <u>detailed</u> suggestions on <u>how</u> you'd <u>perform</u>, <u>design</u> or <u>direct</u> a production to help the examiner <u>visualise</u> your ideas.
- Describe the <u>desired effect</u> of a production on the <u>audience</u>, as well as <u>how</u> this effect might be <u>created</u> using <u>theatrical techniques</u>.

About the Exam

Read the extract carefully before you begin

1) All the exam questions about *The Crucible* will ask you to refer to <u>the extract</u>, so make sure you've <u>fully understood</u> it before you start writing.

2) Some questions will also ask you to write about the <u>play as a whole</u>, so you'll need to <u>relate your ideas</u> about how to stage the extract to other <u>ideas</u> or <u>events</u> in the play.

3) Read each question <u>carefully</u>, then read through the extract. Think about what happens <u>before</u> and <u>after</u> the extract to help you work out how it <u>fits in</u> with the <u>rest</u> of the play. <u>Highlight</u> any <u>important words</u> or <u>phrases</u> (including <u>stage directions</u>). You might also want to <u>annotate</u> the extract as you go along.

4) For <u>shorter answers</u>, you should start writing as soon as you feel <u>comfortable</u> with the extract. But for <u>longer answers</u>, you should <u>plan</u> out a few key <u>ideas</u> for your answers. You could do this by jotting down some <u>bullet points</u> or making a quick <u>diagram</u> (see p.76).

5) Your answer should be <u>coherent</u> — not just a list of <u>different</u> possibilities for the extract. For example, if you start writing about a naturalistic approach, don't <u>swap</u> to a non-naturalistic one <u>halfway through</u>. A good <u>plan</u> will help to make sure your ideas <u>flow</u> and are <u>well-structured</u>.

Shorter answers should be concise

Remember that you shouldn't spend too much time on <u>short-answer</u> questions that aren't worth many marks. Your <u>answers</u> will need to be <u>snappy</u> and <u>straight to the point</u>. Have a look at this example:

Imagine you are a prop designer for a production of *The Crucible*. Suggest some props or stage furniture for the start of Act Three and explain why your choices are appropriate. You should refer to the play's context in your answer.

Turn to p.76-79 for examples of what a longer question and answer might look like.

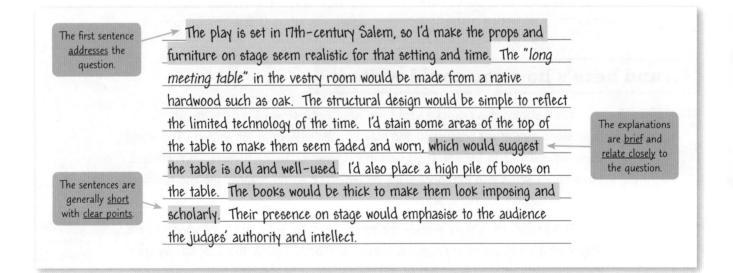

The first sentence <u>addresses</u> the question.

The play is set in 17th-century Salem, so I'd make the props and furniture on stage seem realistic for that setting and time. The "long meeting table" in the vestry room would be made from a native hardwood such as oak. The structural design would be simple to reflect the limited technology of the time. I'd stain some areas of the top of the table to make them seem faded and worn, which would suggest the table is old and well-used. I'd also place a high pile of books on the table. The books would be thick to make them look imposing and scholarly. Their presence on stage would emphasise to the audience the judges' authority and intellect.

The explanations are <u>brief</u> and <u>relate closely</u> to the question.

The sentences are generally <u>short</u> with <u>clear points</u>.

EXAM TIP

Manage your time carefully in the exam...

The questions will be worth different marks in the exam. Make sure you don't spend all your time on questions that are worth fewer marks — plan ahead for roughly how long you should spend on each one.

Sample Question and Answer

Here's an example of how one of the longer questions in your exam could look. You'll need to write about design in quite a bit of detail — take a look at the sample answer on these pages for some tips on what to do.

Here's a sample question about design

Here's what a long question about <u>design</u> might look like:

> You won't have to hunt for the extract in the exam — it'll be printed in your exam paper.

> Find the part of Act Three where Elizabeth denies Proctor's adultery.
> Read from where Danforth says "**And when she put this girl out of your house**"
> to where Elizabeth says "**Oh, God!**", then answer the question below.
>
> Q1 Imagine you are a sound designer working on this extract of *The Crucible*.
> Explain how you would use sound to stage this extract effectively for the audience.

Here's how you could plan your answer...

Music cut off to mark moment of denial ("No sir")

Some non-diegetic sound (to build tension)

Naturalistic style — realistic sounds for realistic setting

Public nature of setting (link to Elizabeth's dilemma)

Pre-recorded muffled voices for location

Music to change volume & pace to reflect rising action

Climax of action

Introduction

Setting

Sound design

Extract after very dramatic moment, still tense

Incidental music, minor key (ominous)

Voices

Tense situation

Knock, heavy thudding (sombre). Slow (anticipation)

Danforth amplified to show power & authority — wireless microphone

Volume of voices — contrast Danforth's power with others (Elizabeth's vulnerability)

... and here's how you could write it

> This describes the <u>overall effect</u> you want to achieve.

When staging this extract, I would use naturalistic sound effects to match the naturalistic style of my production and maintain the realism of the setting. This would allow the audience to become engrossed in the tense exchange between Danforth and Elizabeth. I would also introduce some non-diegetic sound towards the end of the extract to support the rising action.

> This gives <u>an aspect</u> of <u>sound design</u> and explains how it'd be <u>created</u>.

This extract takes place outside the room where the trials are conducted. At the beginning, I would play a pre-recorded audio of muffled voices, made by having actors speak excitedly with cloths over their mouths. It would be directed through speakers on the right-hand side of the theatre. This would suggest the presence of the crowd of people who are in the courtroom, offstage left. When "The door opens" and Elizabeth enters, I would increase the volume of the recording and add reverb to create an echo

> Including <u>technical</u> terms shows a <u>good knowledge</u> of the topic.

effect. This would give the impression that sound is flowing through the door from a larger, adjoining room, highlighting the setting's close proximity to the crowd. As well as establishing the location for the audience, this would also communicate the public

Sample Question and Answer

nature of the setting, which is important for helping the audience to understand the pressure that Elizabeth is under to protect Proctor's reputation later in the extract. I would gradually fade out the recording after Elizabeth enters the room to focus the audience's attention on the actors' dialogue.

This shows a <u>thorough understanding</u> of the extract.

The extract comes immediately after a moment of high tension in the play when Proctor confesses to his affair, so I'd make sure my sound design reflects the tenseness of the situation. The *"knock"* that signals Parris's return would be produced offstage by striking a thick, metal bar against solid wood three times. This would produce a heavy, thudding sound, which would help to maintain a sombre and forbidding mood. I'd also ensure there was a prolonged pause between each knock, which would help to build anticipation among the audience for Elizabeth's arrival on stage. This would increase tension because the audience knows that her questioning will determine Danforth's opinion of Proctor and the integrity of the trials as a whole.

Explain the <u>reasons</u> behind your design choices.

When staging this extract, I'd want to convey the authority that Danforth has over the other characters. I would amplify Danforth's voice using a wireless microphone attached to the actor's costume to make his voice consistently louder than those of the other characters. This difference in volume between Danforth's character and Elizabeth's character when she speaks *"faintly"* would be particularly noticeable, which would also help to highlight the fact that this is the point of the play when Elizabeth's character is most vulnerable. When Danforth gives the commands "Enter!", "Answer my question!" and "Remove her!", I would route his microphone through speakers positioned around the audience to create a surround sound effect. This would make his authority seem more real to the audience and highlight the far-reaching extent of his control in this extract.

This provides specific detail about the <u>equipment</u> that you'd use.

You can use <u>stage directions</u> from the play to support your ideas.

Towards the end of the extract, the action builds to a climax. When Danforth says "Look at me!", a piece of incidental music featuring a fast-paced violin melody in a minor key would be introduced at a low volume. This non-diegetic sound would signify a change in the pace of the action to the audience, and the minor key would hint that something ominous is about to happen. This would create a sense of apprehension for the audience, as they'll be afraid that Elizabeth will reveal Proctor as a liar. I'd build the volume of the music until Danforth has to shout over it. It would reach its maximum volume at the point when Danforth directly confronts Elizabeth by asking if Proctor is a "lecher". This would signify that Danforth's interrogation has reached its dramatic conclusion.

This shows that the answer considers the <u>whole extract</u>.

This uses <u>quotes</u> from the play to clearly indicate <u>when</u> certain effects would be used.

To mark the significance of Elizabeth's denial, I'd cut off the music when Elizabeth says "No, sir." It would then play loudly again, before ending abruptly when the *"door closes"* behind Herrick. The ensuing shocked silence would create a sense of finality to show that Proctor's final hope of being believed has disappeared.

The answer looks at how design <u>supports</u> the <u>action</u> of the extract.

EXAM TIP

I wonder if Parris and Danforth have a secret knock...

It's important to include lots of detail when you're discussing your design ideas. Make sure you use relevant technical terms and describe exactly how you'd create the effects that you're trying to achieve.

Sample Question and Answer

You've seen how to answer a long question about design, but you'll need to write about performance too. This sample answer takes the same extract and looks at it from a character performance point of view.

Here's a sample question about performance

Here's what a long question about <u>performance</u> might look like:

> Find the part of Act Three where Elizabeth denies Proctor's adultery.
> Read from where Danforth says "**And when she put this girl out of your house**" to where Elizabeth says "**Oh, God!**", then answer the question below.
>
> Q1 You are part of a production of *The Crucible*.
> Imagine you're a performer who is playing the role of Elizabeth. Discuss how you would use your performance skills to portray Elizabeth in this extract. You should explain why your ideas are appropriate for this extract, and for the rest of the play.

Here's how you could plan your answer...

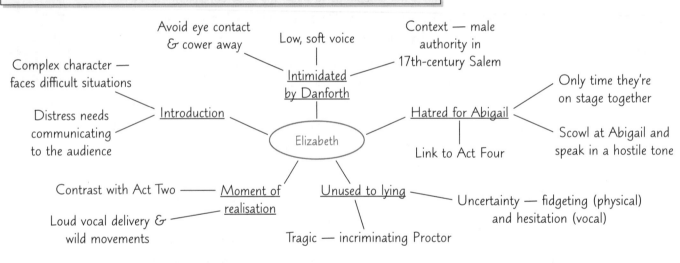

Avoid eye contact & cower away — Low, soft voice — Context — male authority in 17th-century Salem → Intimidated by Danforth

Complex character — faces difficult situations — Distress needs communicating to the audience → Introduction

Hatred for Abigail — Only time they're on stage together — Scowl at Abigail and speak in a hostile tone — Link to Act Four

Elizabeth

Contrast with Act Two — Loud vocal delivery & wild movements → Moment of realisation

Unused to lying — Uncertainty — fidgeting (physical) and hesitation (vocal) — Tragic — incriminating Proctor

... and here's how you could write it

[Keep your introduction <u>brief</u> and <u>focused</u> on the <u>question</u>.]

Elizabeth Proctor is a complex character who deals with a lot of difficult situations throughout the play. A good example of this takes place when she is interrogated by Deputy-Governor Danforth. In this extract, an actor needs to use their performance skills to communicate Elizabeth's distress to the audience.

[This picks out <u>one aspect</u> of the <u>character</u> and explains how it might be <u>performed</u>.]

Throughout the extract, I would choose to show that Elizabeth is intimidated by Danforth's authority and doesn't know how to respond to him. I would communicate this by avoiding eye contact with Danforth and cowering away from him when he moves close. The stage directions state that Elizabeth replies to Danforth's questions "faintly", so I would pause before each line and lower my voice until the audience could only just hear it. This would add to the sense that Elizabeth is uneasy under Danforth's scrutiny.

[This shows that you've considered the play's <u>context</u>.]

This portrayal of Elizabeth would also make her seem weaker and more vulnerable than male authority figures like Danforth, which would reflect the male-dominated nature of 17th-century Puritan society. I would emphasise this point further by using a slightly

Sample Question and Answer

hunched posture to make her look even smaller. In addition, Elizabeth is physically and emotionally exhausted after being accused of witchcraft and arrested. This might partly be reflected in her hunched posture, but I would also use laboured movements and a drawn facial expression to emphasise her exhaustion to the audience.

This shows good awareness of the play as a whole.

This extract is significant in that it is the only time that Elizabeth and Abigail appear on stage together. When Elizabeth enters, the stage directions say that she looks around the room for Proctor, but I would notice Abigail first and scowl at her before doing this. This would reinforce the fact that Elizabeth still feels bitter about the affair, several months after it happened. Later in the extract, when talking about Abigail, I would say "She — dissatisfied me" slowly and in a resentful tone of voice to suggest that Elizabeth is struggling to contain her hatred for Abigail. To add to the sense of hostility, I would almost spit out the name "Abigail Williams". This vocal delivery would imply that Elizabeth blames Abigail as much as Proctor for the affair, which would help to make it even more surprising in Act Four when Elizabeth admits part of the responsibility herself.

The character's back story is key in deciding how to perform them.

Always explain the effect of your performance decisions.

At the end of the extract, Elizabeth makes the difficult decision not to damage Proctor's reputation by revealing his affair with Abigail to the other characters. She is not used to lying, so I would hesitate frequently and stumble over my words when Elizabeth is explaining why she put Abigail "out on the highroad". Soon afterwards, she refers to Proctor as a "goodly man". At this point, I would add emphasis to the word "goodly", as if Elizabeth wants to appear more convincing. However, the stage directions say that she's "in agony" at the time, so I would also fidget nervously and shuffle my feet to express her fear and uncertainty to the audience. This is a pivotal moment in Elizabeth's character development and the play as a whole, because she is torn between defending Proctor and telling the truth. To emphasise the intense pressure that she is feeling, I would let out a pitiful sob after answering "No, sir." This would also make Elizabeth seem helpless and add to the sense of tragedy for the audience, who know that she is incriminating Proctor with these words.

Use short quotes to make it clear to the examiner which part of the extract you're referring to.

You can quote stage directions, but you should add your own ideas to them.

This considers the impact of the portrayal on the audience.

Elizabeth is being led off stage when she finds out that Proctor has already confessed to adultery, but I would draw the audience's attention to her by making her reaction as loud and dramatic as possible. I would shout "Oh, God!" in a loud, high-pitched voice to make Elizabeth sound panicked and show that she has realised the consequences of lying to Danforth. I would also struggle wildly in Herrick's grasp to suggest that she is desperate for a chance to explain herself. This would present a striking contrast to Elizabeth's behaviour in Act Two, where she responds to being arrested in a more dignified way. This change in behaviour would allow the audience to see that Elizabeth is now worried that Proctor's life is at stake, as well as her own.

Make a range of points about vocal and physical skills.

Explain how your choices are either similar or different to the rest of the play.

You'll need to handle the pressure better than Elizabeth...

The longer questions require you to explain your ideas to the examiner in more detail, but that doesn't give you an excuse to waffle — everything you include should still be relevant to the question at hand.

Glossary

antagonist	A character who causes trouble for the protagonist.
backlighting	When the stage is lit from behind to produce silhouettes of the actors.
backstory	The events that have happened to a character before the action of the play.
barndoor	A metal flap that can be attached to a stage lantern and used to shape its light beam.
birdie	A small stage lantern which casts a bright, soft-edged beam of light.
blackout	When the stage lights are turned off between scenes or at the end of a performance.
body language	The way movements, posture and gestures can show how someone feels without speaking.
catharsis	The sense of release felt by an audience when a play makes them feel strong emotions.
climax	The turning point in a play, where tension is at its highest.
communism	A political and social system where property is owned collectively, not by individuals.
convention	A feature of staging, design or performance that is common of its time.
diction	The quality (or clarity) of a performer's vocal expression.
downlighting	When the stage is lit from above to highlight certain characters or cast shadows.
dramatic irony	When the audience knows something that the characters don't.
end-on stage	A proscenium arch stage without the arch to frame it.
exposition	The part of a plot which introduces the main characters and hints at the play's later conflict.
falling action	The part of a plot which settles the conflict (it might contain one last moment of suspense).
floodlight	A type of stage lantern which casts a broad wash of light onto the stage.
flying rig	A piece of equipment that the actors can be suspended from to create the illusion of flight.
form	The type of written drama (e.g. play, opera, musical, pantomime).
fourth wall	The imaginary barrier that separates the audience from the world of the play on stage.
Fresnel spotlight	A type of stage lantern which casts a beam with a softly defined edge.
genre	The type of story a play is telling (e.g. comedy, tragedy).
gel	A piece of coloured, heat-resistant, plastic film used to change the colour of a lantern's beam.
gesture	A movement made by part of the body (e.g. arms, head) to convey a character's emotions.
gobo	A thin, metal disc with shapes cut into it which can be slotted into a lantern to project patterns or images onto the stage or a backdrop.
HUAC	The House Un-American Activities Committee, a US government body that investigated suspected communists in the 1950s. They targeted the entertainment industry in particular.
incidental music	Any music which accompanies a performance and is used to create mood or tension.
inflection	Changes in the pitch and tone of a person's voice as they speak.
intonation	The rise and fall of a performer's voice to create a natural pattern of speech.

Glossary

Glossary

lighting rig	A structure above the stage and wings which holds the stage lanterns.
McCarthyism	Senator McCarthy's campaign to hunt out suspected communists in America in the 1950s.
naturalism	A style of theatre which tries to recreate real life on stage as closely as possible. In contrast, a non-naturalistic style includes features that remind the audience what they're watching isn't real.
posture	The position a character holds themselves in when sitting or standing.
profile spotlight	A type of stage lantern that produces a sharply defined beam. These lanterns are used to focus on a particular character or part of the stage.
promenade theatre	A style of theatre that requires the audience to follow the actors between different performance spaces over the course of the play. This usually takes place outdoors.
prop	An item on stage that the characters can interact with.
proscenium arch stage	A box-shaped stage which is set back from the audience so that only the front end is open to them, framed by the proscenium arch itself.
protagonist	The main character in a story.
proxemics	The use of the physical space between the actors on stage to create meaning.
Puritanism	The beliefs of a group of devout Christians who valued a simple, serious lifestyle and hard work.
resolution	The section of a plot where any loose ends left over from the falling action are tied up.
rising action	The section of a plot which develops the conflict and builds tension.
soundscape	A collection of individual sounds that are layered up to create a strong sense of place.
stage directions	Any instructions written in a script by the playwright to explain how a play should be performed.
stage furniture	Any moveable object on stage which isn't a costume, a prop or a part of the scenery.
strobe	A type of stage lantern which rapidly flashes on and off.
structure	The shape of a play's narrative, including the order in which it's shown to the audience.
style	The way in which a director chooses to interpret a performance text on stage.
subtext	The underlying or hidden meaning behind a character's speech and actions.
symbolism	The use of props, gestures, setting, lighting, etc. to represent other things and create meaning.
theatre in the round	A style of staging which seats the audience on all sides of a central stage.
thrust stage	A stage which extends out into the audience, so that they're standing or sitting on three sides.
tragedy	A genre of play which features a serious plot and an unhappy ending.
tragic hero	The protagonist of a tragedy, whose flaws lead to their downfall (and often their death).
traverse stage	A long, narrow stage which runs between the audience, who face the stage on both sides.
truck	A structure on wheels which can be painted on both sides and used as scenery.
uplighting	When the stage is lit from below to create an unusual or unsettling effect.
wings	The space to the side of a stage which is used for storage and as a waiting area for the actors.

Index

The Characters in 'The Crucible'

Phew! You should be an expert on *The Crucible* by now. But if you want a bit of light relief and a quick recap of the play's plot, sit yourself down and read through *The Crucible — The Cartoon...*

John Proctor

In jail

Elizabeth Proctor

In jail

Abigail Williams

Reverend Parris

Reverend Hale

Thomas and Ann Putnam

Giles Corey

Tituba

Mary Warren

Deputy-Governor Danforth

Rebecca Nurse

In jail

Arthur Miller's 'The Crucible'